113 GALICIAN-PORTUGUESE TROUBADOUR POEMS

This book is part of a series ASPECTS OF PORTUGAL

So far published: Michael Teague: *In the Wake of the Portuguese Navigators* ☐ *CAMÕES* translated by Keith Bosley; illustrated by Lima de Freitas ☐ MAURICE COLLIS: *The Grand Peregrination* ☐ ROSE MACAULAY; *They Went to Portugal Too* ☐ L.M.E. SHAW: *Trade, Inquisition and the English Nation in Portugal 1650-1690* ☐ A.J.R. RUSSELL-WOOD: *A World on the Move* ☐ C.R. BOXER. The following: *The Portuguese Seaborne Empire 1415-1825* ☐ *The Christian Century in Japan 1549-1650* ☐ *The Golden Age of Brazil 1695-1750* ☐ FERNANDO PESSOA: *The Book of Disquietude* translated by Richard Zenith ☐ *A Centenary Pessoa* edited by Eugénio Lisboa with L.C. Taylor ☐ FERNÃO MENDES PINTO: *The Peregrination* translated by Michael Lowery ☐ EÇA DE QUEIROS: The following: *Cousin Bazilio* translated by Roy Campbell ☐ *The Illustrious House of Ramires* translated by Ann Stevens ☐ *The Maias* translated by Patricia McGowan Pinheiro and Ann Stevens ☐ *The Yellow Sofa and Three Portraits* translated by John Vetch and others ☐ *The Sin of Father Amaro* translated by Nan Flanagan ☐ *The City and the Mountains* translated by Roy Campbell ☐ *To the Capital* translated by John Vetch.

113 GALICIAN-PORTUGUESE TROUBADOUR POEMS

Translated by Richard Zenith

CARCANET

in association with

CALOUSTE GULBENKIAN FOUNDATION

INSTITUTO CAMÕES

First published in 1995 by
Carcanet Press Limited
402-406 Corn Exchange Buildings
Manchester M4 3BY

This book belongs to the series *Aspects of Portugal*,
published in Great Britain by Carcanet Press
in association with the Calouste Gulbenkian Foundation,
and with the collaboration of the Anglo-Portuguese Foundation.

Series editors: Eugénio Lisboa, Michael Schmidt, L.C. Taylor

A CIP catalogue record for this book
is available from the British Library
ISBN 1 85754 207 X

The publisher acknowledges financial assistance
from the Arts Council of England

Set in 10 pt Garamond Simoncini by Bryan Williamson, Frome
Printed and bound in England by SRP Ltd, Exeter

Contents

Galician-Portuguese Troubadour Poetry: Introduction

Poetry as Royal Escape

Alfonso X 'the Learned' was one of the greatest royal patrons of scholarship and the arts that the Western world has known. But patron is too small a word, for this monarch did much more than open the lid to the royal treasury or the doors to his palace. While he indeed financed the School of Translators at Toledo, re-established the University of Salamanca, and received the ill-starred troubadours who had fled from persecution in southern France, he also set his own pen to parchment, and not as a mere dilettante. He was a sensitive artist and a discerning scholar, and prolific in both capacities, which is rather amazing when we consider his circumstances. As King of Castile and León from 1252 to 1284, he was by no means immune to the bellicose spirit of the medieval cosmos, having fought back the Moors, having fought against the tiny kingdom of Navarre, having fought for the title of Holy Roman Emperor, and having fought off his throne-hungry brother and son. And yet he found the time and mental concentration to coordinate the production of a *General History*, an unfinished *History of Spain*, treatises on subjects ranging from hunting to the game of chess, a comprehensive legal code, translations from Arabic, Hebrew and Latin, and astronomical tables whose authority went undisputed for hundreds of years after the King's own star had set.

The King's more purely literary achievements were no less impressive. A great supporter of lyric poetry of various sorts and of troubadour poets from various countries, Alfonso X's own poetic compositions rank among the finest of his day and time. And here we come upon a mystery that leads into our subject. The King wrote all his prose in elegant Castilian Spanish, his native tongue, but all his poetry – profane and religious – in Galician-Portuguese, the language which was spoken both inside Portugal and north of it, in the Spanish region of Galicia.[1]

Much has been written to explain this linguistic division of powers, and a number of normally rigorous critics have concluded that Galician-

[1] Modern Galician, although strongly influenced by Spanish, is considered by most linguists to be fundamentally more akin to Portuguese. In the Galician government's effort to standardize the written and (to a lesser extent) spoken tongue, Portuguese is the model whenever there is doubt.

Portuguese had intrinsically 'lyrical' qualities that caused poets in all but the easternmost part of the Peninsula to prefer it over Spanish, its presumably more prosaic cousin. According to this view, Alfonso X simply fell in step with established usage. But how established was Galician-Portuguese as a language of court poetry in central Spain? In the Leonese court of Alfonso X's grandfather, Alfonso IX (ruled 1188-1230), Provençal[2] troubadours such as Giraut de Bornelh and Peire Vidal produced songs in their own tongue, while locals began to compose in Galician-Portuguese, though not exclusively.[3] Galician-Portuguese poetry came into its own in the court of Ferdinand III, Alfonso X's father, who reigned over Castile from 1217, and over Castile and León from 1230 to 1252. It was there – where the crown prince was already poetically active – and in Alfonso X's own court that troubadour songs in Galician-Portuguese began to be produced on a large scale. Far from following an entrenched usage, Alfonso X and his literary cronies were probably responsible for securing Galician-Portuguese's position as the koiné of most court poetry in Iberia.

The lyrical theory of Galician-Portuguese's superiority as a poetic language doesn't fare well in the light of history, the Spanish poetry of succeeding centuries having produced the likes of Juan de Mena, Garcilaso de la Vega, John of the Cross and Góngora, while Galician as a written language gradually sank out of existence until Rosalia de Castro resurrected it in the nineteenth century. (In Portugal, meanwhile, the Galician-Portuguese tongue was forced into the straightjacket of a purer Latin syntax to emerge as modern Portuguese.) But even in Alfonso X's time, there was Gonzalo de Berceo, whose Spanish verses in praise of the Virgin were not inferior to the King's own *Songs in Praise of Holy Mary*, which had little to do with court poetry but which he nonetheless wrote in Galician-Portuguese. It is hard to understand why, particularly if we assume (though it is perhaps an erroneous assumption) that at least some of the Marian songs were meant to circulate among the general public, which was by no means bilingual. Even the élite reading public was probably not all bilingual, for one of the

---

[2] 'Provençal' is used throughout this Introduction in the widest sense, referring not only to the province of Provence but to all of the langue d'oc region where court poetry flourished, to the particular language of that poetry, and to the troubadours responsible for it.

[3] Garcia Mendiz d'Eixo (d.1239), a Portuguese noble exiled in León, composed in the langue d'oc (B 454). He was father to two Galician-Portuguese troubadours, including the talented Fernan Garcia Esgaravunha.

original songbooks (T) provides prose translations into Spanish for 24 out of the first 25 songs.

Alfonso X was under no obligation to encourage a fledgling linguistic tradition and to take it over into the religious sphere. If he sponsored so many Galician-Portuguese troubadours, if he was responsible (as the evidence indicates) for compiling large parts of the anthological songbooks of Galician-Portuguese poetry that have come down to us, if he wrote love poetry, obscene poetry, satirical verse and religious verse in Galician-Portuguese, then it was because this language inspired him – not for its intrinsic poetic properties but because of what it represented for him. For the King and for many others, Galician-Portuguese was a shared private language, a jargon particular to the universe of poetry, the special linguistic support for another dimension, one that was open only to the initiated.

Alfonso X's special attachment to Galician-Portuguese may be partly, albeit speculatively, explained by the fact he was raised in northern Spain, near Burgos, where he was perhaps exposed to the Galician tongue (the ancient kingdom of Galicia having extended eastward along the Bay of Biscay), so that he later associated it with the happier days of his childhood. But the real significance of Galician-Portuguese for troubadour poetry was that it reinforced the artificiality so essential to the genre. In the matter of artifices, the Iberian poets were much less ingenious than their Provençal and French masters, but the simpler songs of the Peninsula – called *cantigas* – had the immediate artificiality of their foreign idiom. Foreign to the hearers, not necessarily to the poets. A majority of the Peninsular troubadours were in fact native to Galicia or northern Portugal, but they more often than not found themselves in Spanish courts, where their nasalized language clearly set them and their *cantigas* apart. Furthermore, the language of the *cantigas* was a modified form of Galician-Portuguese, almost an argot, with a relatively small vocabulary that included a number of Provençal, French and Spanish terms, while certain Galician terms were used in special ways. Let it be noted that the langue d'oc of the Provençal poets was likewise not the same langue d'oc used by the corner grocer. Monosyllables were preferred, words took on new or specialized meanings, and dialectical differences were largely ironed out.

It has been said that romantic love was invented by the Provençal troubadours, and I think this is true insofar as such love be understood as an ideal projected onto an actual or desired or imagined love relationship. The troubadours transferred the feudal concept of vassalage and the Christian idealization of Mary to the beloved's relationship with his lady: he owes her his 'service' as if she were his lord and adores her from a distance like the immaculate and inaccessible Virgin. Certain of the troubadours were no doubt very much 'in love' with their ladies, but these flesh-and-blood women of the court were virtually unrecognizable under the generic, model lady that was projected on them and then venerated in song. The troubadours were thus able to have love – in what they claimed was its most elevated form – quite independently of there being a willing woman, for it was a construction of the troubadour, and any lady would do, even one (indeed, *especially* one) who completely ignored him, impossible loves being the more noble and meritorious.

Besides the love songs known as *cansos*, the Provençal poets also composed sirventes, which commented on society, on political situations or on specific individuals, sometimes with irony or outright satire. The Galician-Portuguese poets took the satiric mode to the heights – or depths – of malice and obscenity. This was nowhere truer than in Alfonso X's court, where the troubadours poked fun at religious figures, political figures (the King included), cowardly soldiers, disloyal nobles, promiscuous women and homosexuals, to name a few of the favourite targets. And they especially liked to cavil among themselves via dialogued *cantigas* known in Provençal as *tensos* – *tenções* in Galician-Portuguese. In the world of their *cantigas* the troubadours could live great loves and great adventures – the crusades, the battles against the Moors, pilgrimages, sexual exploits, verbal duels – without ever lifting a sword, their sexual organs, a foot or a finger, unless this last held a writing instrument. Here was a world in which the world could be rewritten. It was a world of drama and extravagant games, played out with aristocratic detachment. It was high and pure literature: the great escape.

The possibility of escape must have been a great comfort to Alfonso X, most of whose real-life battles foundered. He lost in his bid to be elected Holy Roman Emperor, he failed to make the tiny kingdom of Navarre submit, and he was abandoned by his subjects when his own son rose up against him.[4] If Alfonso X had some initial successes against the Moors it was only because his father, Ferdinand III, had paved the way, and the modest territorial gains were offset by later losses. It was not a happy reign. But in the literary realm the learned King could take

[4] It should be said that the future Sancho IV was justified in his rebellion. His older brother Fernando having died, Sancho was the legitimate heir to the throne, according to the norms of succession set out by Alfonso X. But the King, going against what he himself had established, wanted to pass the crown on to Fernando's son. In 1282, after several years of civil war, Sancho effectively defeated his father, who only held on to the throne thanks to the intervention of Pope Martin IV. Sancho was crowned King upon his father's death in 1284.

great satisfaction or at least profound solace, transforming his defeats into the victory of well-rendered poetry, of which his 'Song of Discomfort' (No. 45) is an outstanding example. The narrator expresses utter disillusion with his life as a knight in arms, and he dreams of leading a simpler existence, selling oil and flour from a small boat that would ply up and down the coast. A number of critics have haggled over whether or not this *cantiga* is autobiographical, thus missing or obscuring the point. Literature is always at some level autobiographical, and here the level is fairly obvious: Alfonso X must have been exceedingly weary of fighting losing battles, and he could hardly avoid feeling dismay over his numerous political and personal setbacks. It does not matter that his outward circumstances were not those of the poem's narrator (described as a sentinel who made rounds), and it's absurd to suppose that he seriously entertained notions of laying aside his crown to become a flour merchant. It would, moreover, have been redundant to do so, for he had already done it, literarily speaking. Poetry had asserted itself as another plane of reality – conditioned by religion and feudal society, but autonomous, transforming, and in a certain way untouchable. The troubadour poetry that began in Provence and spread in all directions – northern France, Germany, Italy and Iberia – was one of the first expressions of the unrelenting individuality that was to shake the Church's foundations via heterodox reform movements and eventually lead to the Renaissance. And I would argue that 'rebirth' is not an entirely felicitous term to the extent it implies revival of old cultural traditions, namely those of the Greeks and Romans. For artists there was indeed a revival of subject matter and procedures, but there was also something completely new: the first centuries of this millennium witnessed the birth of a mentality that had never existed.

If this Introduction has dwelled on one individual to present a school of poetry and song that included over 150 troubadours and spanned the course of 150 years, it is not only to highlight Alfonso X's crucial role for the full flowering of Galician-Portuguese poetry: it is also to make the point that this was a literature of, by, and for individuals, unlike any literature ever before produced in the Western world. Compositions were signed, they belonged to identifiable authors, and in the songbooks of the Provençal troubadours we even find biographies introducing the poets. The epic literature that preceded theirs (and continued to flourish alongside it) was the expression of a people, and the escape it afforded was into a collective imagination, not unlike the escape offered by religion. Indeed, religion and literature often overlapped, and for the Greeks they were inseparable. It was of course individuals who produced Greek drama, but their tragedies and comedies were extracted from the social sphere and the commonly shared rather than from personal experience. The troubadours, in contrast, were anti-tragic, intimate to the point of obscurity, and rarely lofty in tone. They made their poems for other members of their fairly exclusive club, or for just one other person, or for their own satisfaction, and this seems to have been a new motivation for producing literature. Greek and Roman poets expressed personal sentiments, but sincerely, and usually as professionals. The troubadours, on the other hand, made insincerity into an art, and amateurs were welcome. The topics of troubadour poetry were of the most ordinary, or were mere inventions, and while the jongleurs who sang the troubadours' songs were professionals, the troubadours themselves were usually nobles or clerics. The most prolific Galician-Portuguese troubadour was King Dinis of Portugal, and like Alfonso X before him he led a kind of double life in his poetry, drawing from his experience but also reshaping and amplifying that experience. Greek and Roman poetry introduce an impressive array of themes and types, and Ovid is intensely present in the work of Arnaud Daniel, Fouquet de Marseille and others, so I would not wish to insist too much on the originality of troubadour poetry, but coming at the historical moment when it did, I think it is fair to consider it the point of departure for literature as an expression of individual consciousness and as a vehicle for enlarging that consciousness.

Times, Places, Numbers and Origins

About 1680 Galician-Portuguese *cantigas* have come down to us in three main songbooks containing lyrics but not, unfortunately, any music. The *cantigas* were composed from around the year 1200 to 1350, by poets from all over the Iberian Peninsula, but especially from Galicia and Portugal. In the eastern kingdom of Aragon, which had closer ties with its neighbour across the Pyrenees, court poetry began to be produced already in the mid-twelfth century, but in the langue d'oc, which continued to be used there into the fourteenth century, even after Ramon LLull (1233?-1316?) and others began writing verses in Catalan, which was strongly influenced by the langue d'oc.

While some examples of Galician-Portuguese *cantigas* can be found in the Baena Songbook, a collection of lyric poetry written towards the end of the fourteenth century and the beginning of the fifteenth, predominantly in Spanish, most scholars accept 1350 as the terminus for the Galician-Portuguese school. In that year the Count of Barcelos, a bastard son of King Dinis (1279-1325), made out a will that assigned the *Book of Cantigas* to Alfonso XI, King of Castile and León (1312-1350).

This book was probably the compilation of *cantigas* from which two of the three surviving Songbooks derived.

The starting point for the Galician-Portuguese school is a harder matter. Scholars have variously proposed 1189, 1196, 1209 and 1213 as the date for the oldest surviving *cantiga*, and there is disagreement about just which *cantiga* is the oldest. An infinitely tougher question is whether the oldest surviving *cantigas* were in fact the oldest to be composed. Were there earlier manuscripts that have been lost? Or was there an oral culture on the Peninsula which, like the monuments and the palaces of nobles, left no traces?

That there was a tradition of folk song passed down orally from generation to generation can hardly be doubted, but was there an oral tradition of court poetry? Probably not. The Galician-Portuguese court poetry that has survived is a frank imitation of Provençal and northern French models, more or less modified by the influence of a native folk music that was sung by humble women or at least sung from their point of view. This gave rise to the most original contribution of the Galician-Portuguese school, the *cantigas d'amigo*, in which a humble girl typically pines after her absent lover. Long before the troubadours appeared on the scene, travelling bards no doubt frequented the Iberian courts, but if there existed a lyrical genre specific to the courts, how explain that it left no visible mark on the poetry imported from France, even though the native folk poetry left a very definite imprint? At the most we might suppose that Galician-Portuguese court poetry began to be composed in the mid-twelfth century, when the first Provençal troubadours arrived from across the Pyrenees. But the evidence suggests that, as happened in Aragon and Catalonia, the local poets in León and Castile initially imitated not only the form but the language of the Provençal poets, composing songs in the langue d'oc. On the other hand, the earliest recorded verses in Galician-Portuguese may well belong to Raimbaut de Vaqueiras, a Provençal troubadour who flourished towards the end of the twelfth century. He wrote a *descort* in five languages, one of which seems to be Galician-Portuguese, though several of the verses more nearly resemble Aragonese or Castilian Spanish. Before drawing conclusions about the significance of these verses, we should consider the fact that this same troubadour may have also written the first verses in an Italian tongue. At a time when Sordello (mentioned by Dante) and other Italians were writing court poetry in the langue d'oc, Raimbaut de Vaqueiras wrote a bilingual poem in which a Provençal jongleur courts a Genoese lady who tells him in her native dialect to get lost. If there were already existing court poetries in Italian and in Galician-Portuguese, it seems a bizarre coincidence that the oldest surviving examples of both might belong to a troubadour from Provence. More likely is that this playful polyglot, fond of hybrid linguistic and literary games (he also wrote a Peninsular-inspired *cantiga d'amigo* in the langue d'oc), produced troubadour poetry in other languages as an experiment, when virtually nothing of the sort yet existed.[5] The oldest surviving *cantigas* may very well be the oldest ones produced. I would also contend that court poetry, far from being orally elaborated and passed on, was written down at the time of composition, and that this was yet another way in which it differed from the poetry that preceded it.

It should be immediately stressed that Galician-Portuguese troubadour poetry, perhaps even more than its Provençal progenitor, was tremendously indebted to oral tradition. The repertoire of themes and poetic devices that characterize the Galician-Portuguese school resulted from the marriage of a pre-existing folk poetry with Provençal court poetry, which in turn owed a debt (of indeterminate size) to the oral song tradition of southern France. For reasons that are not entirely clear, the song tradition on the Iberian Peninsula was particularly strong in Galicia, and even into the nineteenth century we find passages in travel journals that marvel over the vibrant culture of song among the Galicians. Of course, such testimonies could probably be found for every other region in Spain. Is there any culture in the world that can't boast of a musical tradition? The enormous influence of Galician song on the rest of the Peninsula was probably due not to its musical superiority but to the role it played in Santiago de Compostela, whose massive cathedral, completed in the 1130s, became the most visited shrine west of Rome, with as many as two million pilgrims from France and elsewhere flocking there yearly to pay homage to St James.

Galicia was on the whole an impoverished region and had no royal court, but Santiago – its jewel – was for several hundred years the richest, most powerful and most international city on the Peninsula. The hordes of pious visitors naturally had to be lodged, fed and otherwise provided for, and so a somewhat less godly infrastructure evolved. There were innkeepers, tavernkeepers, money exchangers, sellers of

---

[5] The three Vaqueiras texts are published in Riquer, v.I, pp.840-842 ('Eras quan vey verdeyar'), pp.816-819 ('Domna, tant vos ai preiada'), and pp.843-844 ('Altas undas que venez suz la mar'). The first of these, the *descort*, consists of five 8-line stanzas in Provençal, Italian, French, Gascon and an adulterated form of Galician-Portuguese, with a final 10-line stanza consisting of two verses from each language. The fact that neither Gascon nor Italian were literary languages discredits the 'proof' of Galician-Portuguese's literary status on the basis of what is after all a substandard example.

souvenirs, thieves on the lookout for unwary tourists, knights to protect the tourists from said thieves, and a whole array of entertainers to keep everyone amused when the day's devotions were over or when the flesh simply grew weak. It is easy to imagine the kind of bacchanalia that ran parallel to the religious activities with more or less equal fervour. (The last stanza of No. 96 suggests as much.) And in both spheres – religious and secular – song was a preeminent mode of expression. The Galician-Portuguese hymnal was far more extensive than any other on the Peninsula, and while Latin was the language of sacred music, much of which was imported from Cluny and other French monasteries, we find traces of the local dialect. The music itself had roots that went far back, Galicia's Christians having driven out the Moors early on, and there are ancient hymns whose prosody resembles that of certain *cantigas* of the troubadours. It is only natural that pilgrims, even the pious ones (and many were not at all pious, having been forced to make the pilgrimage as a penance for some crime, or having been attracted out of curiosity or the desire to travel), would have a lot of free time that needed to be filled, and profane music was no doubt in high demand. Attending to the pilgrim tourists was one of the pillars of the local economy, and nothing was free of charge. Singers became professionalized, and they were not averse to travelling to wherever their services would be compensated, and what more attractive place than the royal courts, whose relatively comfortable lifestyle might in itself be sufficient compensation? Towards the end of the twelfth century, when Santiago began to decline in popularity, many musicians had no choice but to find work elsewhere. Experienced and cosmopolitan, they probably had little difficulty in adapting the new style of Provençal song to their own native music, which by that time had already spread across much of Spain and Portugal, at least in the courts of kings and rich nobles.

Like the minstrels of Santiago, the Provençal troubadours also travelled for economic reasons, going wherever they were well received, and the generous courts of Spain were a favoured destination. Their travels intensified toward the end of the twelfth century, when the popularity of court poetry had already peaked in southern France, and after 1209 they began to emigrate for political-religious reasons, being persecuted by the Church (via a crusade and then the Inquisition), which associated them with the Albigensian heresy.

Marcabrun and other Provençal troubadours began to visit Castile and León already in the time of Alfonso VII, who ruled over the two kingdoms from 1126 to 1157. During the political split that followed, the troubadours were as welcome as ever, Alfonso VIII of Castile (ruled 1158-1214) taking in twenty or more under his wing, while Alfonso IX of León (cited above) seems to have done some poetizing himself. But it was after reunification, in 1230, that the court of Ferdinand III became a veritable breeding ground for Galician-Portuguese poetry, the intense contact between troubadours from Provence and minstrels from Galicia and Portugal finally producing the fully autonomous, hybrid form that is Galician-Portuguese court poetry – less sophisticated than its Provençal and French counterparts, but presenting original aspects and adapting foreign models in an original way. Alfonso X, heir to the throne, was already very much active in the new poetic school.

Although we may reasonably argue that the ardent literary activity of the Castilian and Leonese monarchs enabled Galician-Portuguese poetry to evolve into a true school, with topics and formal procedures that distinguished it from the Provençal school, it is the Portuguese court that seems to have been the cradle of the new poetry. The Galician-Portuguese songbooks, unlike the Provençal ones, rarely provide biographical information about the authors, but the earliest identifiable troubadours were for the most part members of the Portuguese nobility, headed by the illustrious name of Sancho I, Portugal's king from 1185 to 1211. The Portuguese royal house – less wealthy and less ostentatious than the Spanish houses, and farther removed from the rest of Europe – did not attract Provençal troubadours in great numbers, but Portugal had strong connections with France from the very foundation of its national identity. It was under Count Henri of Burgundy that the region around Oporto, known as Portucale, became independent in 1095. As he and then his son, Afonso Henriques, asserted their control and pushed the Moors southward, colonists were brought in from Flanders and from northern and southern France. Afonso proclaimed himself King in 1140 and six years later married Mafalda of Savoy, where the langue d'oc was spoken. Given their French origins and their ongoing contact with Provençal and French culture, it is safe to assume that the first Portuguese monarchs were well acquainted with troubadour poetry (which by the mid-twelfth century had spread to northern France), and it is likely that they brought at least a few troubadours to their courts.

But if the first Galician-Portuguese troubadour poems were produced in the kingdom of Portugal, how explain King Dinis's wish – almost a century later – to make a song of love 'in Provençal style', as if this were something novel? Provençal poetry had in fact already fallen out of favour, and yet Dinis, who stepped on to the throne in 1279, diligently studied and imitated its forms in many of his 137 surviving *cantigas*. Could it be that that famous national trait known as *saudade*, an endlessly wistful longing for the past, had already taken hold in the Portuguese? Whatever the case, Dinis's court – the first lavish court in

Portugal – was the other great centre for the Galician-Portuguese school, with many poets transferring there from the Castilian court after Alfonso X's death in 1284. After Dinis's death in 1325, the old-fashioned troubadour poetry disappeared forthwith, on the Peninsula as in the rest of Europe, but it left a heritage that in seven centuries has never been threatened. Lyric poetry had taken its place in the modern world as a *personal* mode of expression, of protest, and of reinvention, and it had also affirmed itself as an anti-world, or alternate world: an ever-available, sublime escape.

Structures, Patterns, Devices and Genres

A casual glance through the Galician-Portuguese Songbooks, without reading or understanding a word, will already reveal a common characteristic: the *cantigas* are almost all short but not too. Three or four stanzas of from two to seven verses is the general rule. The same casual glance will also reveal the frequent appearance of a closing couplet or triplet. Termed a *fiinda* in the *Art of Troubadour Poetry [Arte de Trobar]*, a fragmentary treatise found at the beginning of the Songbook of the National Library of Lisbon, these closing verses recall the Provençal *tornada* or envoi, in which the troubadour typically sends his song to a protector or to his lady, who is often designated by a pseudonym (the *senhal*). A *fiinda*, however, merely concludes the argument of the *cantiga*, sometimes in the form of a punch line. In rare cases, the *fiinda* may consist of a single verse or of more than the customary two or three, and some *cantigas* have more than one *fiinda*.

Looking more closely at the *cantigas* in the Songbooks, we will find that a majority have refrains, a legacy from the native song tradition. The texts without refrains are known as *cantigas* of 'mastery' – *meestria* – for they require greater thematic development and technical skill, although they never attain the complexity of the Provençal songs they emulate. The *cantigas* with refrains more often than not have six verses with three rhymes following an abbaCC pattern or, occasionally, an ababCC pattern, in which CC is the refrain. The songs of *meestria* generally have seven verses with three rhymes following one of various patterns, abbacca being the most frequent.

Poor in strophic variety, the *cantigas* also present a reduced number of metrical schemes. Lines of seven or eight syllables are common enough, but fully half of the *cantigas* employ the decasyllable, usually with a masculine rhyme (final syllable stressed). The Galician-Portuguese poets, like the Provençal and the French, counted to the last accented syllable, but they were less rigorous in their counting, with verses that often had one syllable too many or too few. And while they occasionally succeeded in keeping the same rhymes from stanza to stanza (as in No. 104 and No. 105, where it was not by coincidence that King Dinis invoked Provençal poetry), usually they preserved only the pattern.

If in many formal aspects the Galician-Portuguese school seems a dim reflection of Provençal virtuosity, it picks up some lustre with its fascinating, original use of parallelism. Parallelism can be loosely defined as 'repetition with a difference', and it takes several forms, the most poetically effective of which is the literal or linguistic variety, based on the principle of *leixa-pren* [leave-take]. Typically found in *cantigas* with refrains, it is well exemplified in No. 99, by Pero Meogo:

[Levou-s'a louçana,] levou-s'a velida:
vay lavar cabelos, na fontana fria.
Leda dos amores, dos amores leda.

[Levou-s'a velida,] levou-s'a louçana:
vay lavar cabelos, na fria fontana.
Leda dos amores, dos amores leda.

Vay lavar cabelos, na fontana fria:
passou seu amigo, que lhi ben queria.
Leda dos amores, dos amores leda.

Vay lavar cabelos, na fria fontana:
passa seu amigo, que a muyt'amava.
Leda dos amores, dos amores leda.

Passa seu amigo, que lhi ben queria:
o cervo do monte a áugua volvia.
Leda dos amores, dos amores leda.

Passa seu amigo, que a muyt'amava:
o cervo do monte volvia a áugua.
Leda dos amores, dos amores leda.

The even-numbered stanzas repeat the information presented in the odd-numbered stanzas, but with slight variations, end words being substituted by synonyms – *velida* [fair] → *louçana* [pretty], *queria* [liked] → *amava* [loved] – or else changing position – *fontana fria* → *fria fontana* [cold spring], *a áugua volvia* → *volvia a áugua* [stirred the water]. At first glance the even stanzas might appear identical to the odd ones preceding them, but the lines are never exactly the same. On the other hand, a line from each stanza is repeated verbatim two stanzas down, but with a displacement: the second lines of the first two stanzas become the first lines of stanzas three and four, whose second lines in turn become the first lines of stanzas five and six. The verbal house of mirrors is topped off by a refrain in which *Leda dos amores* [Happy with love] re-echoes in inverse form as *dos amores leda*.

The ensemble of these poetic restatements has a mesmerizing effect, heightening the listener's (and nowadays the reader's) sense of the girl's rapture and innocence. It is as if the simple meeting of a girl with her lover were taking place on an otherworldly plane. This may seem an overstatement, but less so when we explore – as some critics have – the symbolic resonance of the water, hair and mountain stag occupying the stage.

Semantic parallelism, which is the repetition not of words but of ideas or subject matter, is well illustrated by No. 2 and No. 72. In these songs there is little or no narrative progress; the first stanza contains the whole story, and successive stanzas merely repeat the information in other words. While this kind of parallelism can dramatize the gravity of a particular feeling or predicament, it risks being tedious.

The *Art of Troubadour Poetry* describes other poetic devices, explained here in the notes to *cantigas* where they are used: No. 75 for a characteristic usage of enjambement *(ata a fiinda)*, No. 66 for the 'missing rhyme' *(palavra perduda)*, No. 73 for word doubling *(dobre)* and No. 21 for modified word doubling *(mozdobre)*. The poetic treatise also describes several modes – dialogued and imitative – that can be applied to one or more of the three major types of songs: *cantigas d'amigo, cantigas d'amor,* and *cantigas d'escarnho*.

CANTIGAS D'AMIGO

The 500 or so songs within this group, close to a third of the Galician-Portuguese output, represent the school's most original component. Nearly always narrated by young, unmarried girls, the *amigo* of these *cantigas* is usually mentioned in the opening lines and may refer to a boyfriend, a lover, a would-be boyfriend or lover, or someone the girl would like as her boyfriend or lover. More often than not the girl is lamenting the *amigo*'s absence, either to herself, her mother, her sisters or her friends, but sometimes she addresses him directly. The origins of the female love lyric on the Peninsula are obscure, but the tradition was evidently extensive, with a number of defining characteristics, and it was present from the start among the Galician-Portuguese troubadours, so that they were almost surely not the first men to appropriate it. Galician minstrels of the twelfth century must have already availed themselves of the women's songs, but why? Because of a demand for them in Santiago and other urban centres, where the bucolic themes and settings were a novelty? Or did the novelty consist in men taking the part of women? Did they even dress for the part?

Girls' songs were not unique to the Iberian Peninsula. There was the ancient *chanson de femme* in France, adapted to the new style by Richart de Fournival (thirteenth century) and other trouvères; and German court poetry – from the Kürenberger (twelfth century) through Neidhart von Reuenthal (d.1246) and other Minnesinger – incorporated a *Mädchenlied* tradition that went back at least to the time of Charlemagne, when nuns and abbesses are known to have written *wineleodes* (*wine* = friend, *leod* = to sing). None of these early conventual lyrics have survived, but the fact they were actually *written*, perhaps for or about men that the nuns had no access to, suggests that poetry as an individual creative act, while 'coming out of the closet' (or cloister?) with the troubadours, already existed among these celibate women, who, dissatisfied with the secular world and not entirely satisfied with the religious world, invented yet a third world of imagined, literary loves.

The *cantigas d'amigo*, on the other hand, proceeded out of a collective, indubitably oral tradition. Even after passing through the moulds of Provençal-inspired court poetry, the overwhelming majority of them kept the refrain that is typical of folk music,[6] and a number of them mention dancing. It was the *cantigas d'amigo* that brought parallelism into the Galician-Portuguese school, and the *leixa-pren* repetition of lines (see above) – found also in liturgical chant – suggests a responsory type of singing. If nothing else, the repeated verses would at least have been an aid to memory before songs began to be written down.

The *cantigas d'amigo* are in a certain way ritualistic, presenting concise moments of intense drama on an open stage: the outdoor world common to all. The woods, streams, lakes, meadows, and especially the seaside – rarely mentioned in Provençal poetry – are typical places where the girl longs or waits for her beloved, or perhaps actually meets him. Sometimes the setting is a local shrine in Galicia or Portugal, but there is nothing religious about the songs, which probably have their roots in pre-Christian times. Just as the celebrated pilgrimage to Santiago

---

[6] The surviving examples of musical notation suggest that these refrains were not, however, sung in chorus, as many scholars have supposed.

was an opportunity for other things besides prayer and devotion, so the smaller religious festivals were (and still are) the occasion for general merriment and amorous encounters, as documented by No. 68, in which the narrator says: 'Come on, girls, let's go to the shrine, where we can dance for our boyfriends while our mothers burn candles for themselves and for us.' The girl, by the way, was not necessarily being cynical. In dialogued *cantigas d'amigo*, the mother may reveal her suspicions or concern over her daughter's enamoured state (No. 8, No. 67, No. 98), or she may actually collaborate with her daughter No. 91).

These themes are centuries away from the scenario of courtly love as conceived in southern France, and while much of the troubadour phraseology – feudal notions of 'service', 'homage', and 'consideration' – was applied to the *cantigas d'amigo*, there are two large pieces of evidence that lead us to believe that the Galician-Portuguese troubadours not only incorporated themes from the female folk tradition but actually 'lifted' verses or entire songs from it. For one thing, the *cantigas d'amigo* contain a number of words that were already archaic in the thirteenth century; for another, they often employ assonance instead of perfect rhyme, definitely out of keeping with orthodox troubadour technique. Strangely enough, there seems to have been a resurgence of the *cantiga d'amigo* towards the end of the thirteenth century, when the Galician-Portuguese school was about to begin its decline, and the specimens produced by King Dinis and other late troubadours still contained ancient words and imperfect rhymes. It would seem, therefore, that the Galician-Portuguese poets continued to rework existing folk songs – perhaps out of a concern to preserve traditional culture?

The origins of the Iberian female song tradition have been hotly debated since 1948, when Samuel Stern published translations of some twenty Mozarabic *kharjas, carjas, jarchas, hardjas, jaryas, khargias, harjat,* or *kharağat*, which are eight versions of the same word, depending on who has done the transliterating from Arabic. The *kharja* was a 'surprise' stanza of 2-4 lines tacked on to the end of a lyric poem known as a *muwaššaha* (also written as *moaxafa, moaxaha, muywashah, muaxáa*), composed by Hebrew and Arabic poets in Andalusia from at least the eleventh through thirteenth centuries. The surprise of the *kharja* was partly in its content – often erotic or at least suggestive – and partly in its language, vulgar Arabic or Mozarabic, sharply contrasting with the Hebrew or classical Arabic of the *muwaššaha*. Mozarabic, which was the Romance tongue of the Christians living under Moorish domination, had many Latin-derived words in common with Spanish and Galician-Portuguese, and the translated Mozarabic *kharja* turned out to be similar in certain respects to the *cantigas d'amigo*. The speaker in the *kharja* is also a woman who laments her love, often because the lover is going or has gone away, and she may address her mother, her sisters, girl friends, or the lover himself. The *kharjas* are more primitive in form, and the love described is more carnal, but most scholars agree there is a relation between the two genres. There is rather less agreement on the nature of the relation. For some, the Mozarabic *kharjas* are evidence that the *cantigas d'amigo* derived from Arabic poetry. More likely, I think, is that the *kharjas* derived from an indigenous poetry that also gave rise to the *cantigas d'amigo* as they existed before troubadour poetry arrived at the Peninsula. And even a completely separate evolution of the two poetries would not be such a strange coincidence: an oriental version of the *cantiga d'amigo* can be found in the Chinese *Book of Songs*, compiled several thousand years ago. Strange, rather, would be the relatively advanced culture in which erotic desire fails to find expression in poetry.

Whatever the origin of the *cantigas d'amigo* and however strong the female song tradition in Galicia, the transforming impact of troubadour models should not be underestimated. If some of the earlier *cantigas d'amigo* (No. 1, No. 6, No. 7, No. 8) seem naive enough, there is nothing innocent about the girl in No. 59 who doesn't believe a word of the suitor who supposedly wants a private meeting 'just to talk'. The girl in No. 60 affirms that her lover's praise is only to be expected, for she's good-looking and deserves it. And the narrator of No. 30 is probably not a girl but a mature woman, who warns other women never to believe the suitor who claims to be dying of love, for she's never yet seen it happen, though she'd certainly like to. These and many other *cantigas d'amigo* were entirely the original work of troubadours, owing more to Provençal poetry than to any indigenous lyrical form.

CANTIGAS D'AMOR

Directly derived from the Provençal *canso*, the *cantiga d'amor* was much appreciated in the Iberian courts as a novel and prestigious cultural item, but a twentieth-century sensibility is apt to prefer the sparer, more evocative style of the *cantigas d'amigo*. In her monumental edition of the Ajuda Songbook, Carolina Michaëlis de Vasconcelos wrote (v.II, p.598) that 'the *cantigas d'amor* [...] are tremendously monotonous, sterile and conventional in their ideas, expressions and metrical forms.' One may marvel that, notwithstanding, the eminent scholar dedicated most of her professional life to studying the *cantigas d'amor*, or perhaps it's that so much study provoked her feeling of monotony. It is fairly standard for critics to disdain the poetic qualities of the *cantigas d'amor*, which are technically less brilliant and thematically less varied than the Provençal prototype, but if we selectively pass over about half of the 700 surviving examples, we are left with a body of texts that presents considerable interest and variety. (I dare say that the same procedure could be applied with profit to almost any general poetry anthology and especially non-contemporary ones, whose compilers were not guided by the same aesthetic taste that guides us.)

Historians no longer affirm that feudalism never existed in the western half of Iberia, but most agree that it was a less powerful and less extensive institution there than it was north of the Pyrenees. In fact the Iberian variety, except in Aragon and Catalonia, should probably not be called an institution. It did not use the feudal jargon in a systematic way, and while relations of vassalage were common enough, the associated rituals of homage (*immixtio manuum*, the oath of fidelity, the formal kiss) were nonessential or nonexistent. Knowing but a pale version of the feudal relation of lord and vassal, the Galician-Portuguese troubadours could produce no better than a pale version of the *canso* that was founded on that relation. They addressed the lady of their *cantigas d'amor* as *senhor* (later feminized to become the modern *senhora* of Portuguese and *señora* of Spanish), but they lacked a clear notion of the homage they owed this 'lord' or of the benefit she owed him. The Provençal troubadour compared the beauty of his lady *(midons)* to nature's most splendid phenomena, and he invested her with the qualities of a powerful and life-giving lord; the Peninsular poet merely accentuated his *senhor(a)*'s ladylike virtues, pouring on limp adjectives like 'fair', 'well-shaped', 'chaste', 'sensible', 'discreet', and 'worthy'. Provençal love is condemned to frustration because the object of love is a perfect ideal that would, if it yielded, become less than perfect, but the poet can at least delight in his praise of that perfection and can realize love on paper, as it were; the Galician-Portuguese poet never achieves such a sublime projection, so that his focus turns back on himself ('Poor me!'), and his rejected love knows no transcendence.

Courtly love becomes the occasion for an obsessive sadness in the Galician-Portuguese domain. The playful and exultant spirit of langue d'oc poetry – its *joi*! – gives way to a self-pitying litany of love's depressing effects. The poet loses sleep, goes insane, or (and this is the all too common trope) dies on account of his love. But he is not necessarily complaining, and he may feel a genuine contentment: pride in his suffering. King Dinis admitted (in No. 105) that the Provençal poets were expert versifiers, but he held up his greater inner torment as proof that his love was more sincere. Nationalistic critics have echoed this argument on behalf of their forefathers who wrote *cantigas d'amor*, and it is true to the extent love implies self-absorption in one's own feeling.

Indeed it was this kind of sincerity that made for a lot of infelicitous poetry among the *cantigas d'amor*. But King Dinis was also able to focus all his attention on the lady, as in No. 104, a panegyric worthy of the Provençal poets and, significantly, a song which Dinis identifies as being 'in Provençal style'. Other Galician-Portuguese troubadours, from the early Pai Soarez de Taveirós (No. 3) to the late Vidal (No. 112) describe their ladies in original, concrete terms, and Joam Garcia de Guilhade has a unique love song about a green-eyed lady (No. 26). This same Guilhade, highly ironic and a disdainer of clichés, offers a nonconforming *cantiga d'amor* (No. 31) in which, after first making mention of the men who say they would die for love, he exclaims:

But, my lady, while I may see you,
I will always want to live
and wait and see!

And there is nothing sad about Airas Nunez, who in the fourteen lines of No. 97 celebrates his love with a euphoric array of images from nature, which he hails as his inspiration for creating verses.

The mirror of Provençal poetry can give only a partial view of the *cantigas d'amor*, whose fundamental structure was modified by the Peninsula's native poetic tradition. They became shorter, often had refrains, and began to employ parallelistic structures. These were traits common to the *cantigas d'amigo*, of course, and No. 90 is in every respect a *cantiga d'amigo* except for its male point of view. No. 4, on the other hand, with its primitively repeating verses, suggests there may have been a pre-troubadour tradition of men's love poetry in Galician-Portuguese. Seven *cantigas*, two of which (No. 62 and No. 108) are presented here, have been identified as pastorals, although purist criticism does not admit the label, for they depart somewhat from the orthodox Provençal or French variety, which features a troubadour in dialogue with a shepherdess. The Galician-Portuguese *pastorelas* generally present the shepherdess in soliloquy, perhaps observed by the troubadour. But No. 62 does include dialogue, as well as an image that seems to have been borrowed from a Provençal pastoral (see the Note to the poem). The Galician-Portuguese pastorals, narrative poems that do not conveniently fit into the *cantiga d'amigo* or *cantiga d'amor* category (I would place them in the latter), are yet another imported form that was 'Peninsularized' into something rather different but not necessarily inferior. Of course, 'not necessarily' is another way of saying 'only sometimes'.

CANTIGAS D'ESCARNHO E MAL DIZER

If the *cantigas d'amor* on the whole lack the splendour of the Provençal *cansos*, they are more than made up for by the magnificent, multifarious, now hilarious, now subtle, now vindictive, now good-humoured, now filthy, now sacrilegious, now instructive, now utterly nasty songs of mockery and slander, one of whose targets is the *cantiga d'amor* itself. Pero Garcia Burgalês, for example, inverts the rules of courtly love in No. 83 by telling a certain Maria Negra that she must feel very lucky to be in love with him. This same Burgalês, mocking fellow troubadour Roi Queimado for repeatedly dying of love (a practice, incidentally, that originated with the Provençal poets, though they did not so abuse it) tells us in No. 82 that 'he died for [his lady] in a refrain, but three days later was back again,' a feat unheard of since the time of Christ. Joam Garcia de Guilhade, when hounded by a lady for a *cantiga d'amor*, complied with No. 33, whose first stanza goes:

Ugly lady, you've complained
that I never sing your praise,
so I've composed a new refrain
telling all your charms that slay me,
and this is what my heart exclaims:
you're a crazy, old and ugly lady!

The Art of Troubadour Poetry (Section 3, Chapters 5-6) distinguishes between two satiric genres by what would seem a simple formula: *de mal dizer* [slander] when the *cantiga* uses straightforward language; *d'escarnho* [same Germanic origin as the English *scorn*] when equivocal terms and double-entendre are employed. In practice the distinction is largely untenable. Guilhade straightforwardly calls the unsung lady ugly, but in the third and fourth lines he uses equivocal language. Satire by definition employs irony, the language of which can never be wholly straightforward. There are of course degrees of irony, and perhaps the troubadour poets knew where to draw the line between the two satiric genres. Modern scholars do not, however, and I've followed their practice of grouping all the satiric verse under a single heading, shortened to *cantigas d'escarnho*.

In connection with the two satiric genres, the *Art of Troubadour Poetry* also makes mention of the *joguete d'arteyro* and the *risabelha*, obscure terms which may refer to pre-existing types. There are no direct proofs of a native tradition of satiric poetry on the Peninsula, but it is tempting to postulate one. Could it be that the pre-troubadour minstrels radiating out from Santiago de Compostela made satiric songs about the hypocrites that flocked there among the truly devout? Religious hypocrisy is one of the themes of the *cantigas d'escarnho* (e.g. No. 22, No. 49), but that is naturally to be expected in a corpus of 400 satiric texts on varied subjects. What surprises is that satire flourished with such brio in the Galician-Portuguese school, for once being more daring and more concrete than its Provençal counterpart.

The Provençal poets expressed satire in the sirvente, of which four types can be distinguished: moral/religious, political, literary, and personal. The last of the four types was sometimes vitriolic, particularly when it mocked inept jongleurs, but the sirvente usually remained dignified. Some of the Galician-Portuguese poets produced moral sirventes à la Provençal, reflecting on the worsening state of the world (No. 14 and No. 15), for example, or on the disappearance of truth (No. 96), but the majority of the *cantigas d'escarnho* are replete with invective, sarcasm and obscenity that transgress the comparatively restrained boundaries of the langue d'oc satirical models. M. Rodrigues Lapa, organizer of the only complete edition of the *cantigas d'escarnho*, called their ensemble a 'moral sewer' (in *Lições*, p.181), and though his is no doubt an old-maidish judgment, many a modern reader or listener will blush at Afons'Eanes do Coton's wonderment that a certain Marinha doesn't explode from the impact of his sexual parts so completely filling hers (No. 12), or at Pero Garcia Burgalês's account of Maria Negra, who goes broke from buying penises that rot as soon as she 'sticks them in her stable' (No. 84). Verses like these – along with others that mock homosexuals (No. 85, No. 86, No. 87), exorbitant prostitutes (No. 13, No. 64), unchaste nuns and priests (No. 11, No. 111), and stupid or boring individuals (No. 25, No. 103) – are cited by certain critics as proof of the Peninsula's lower cultural level, apparently on the assumption that high culture has no room for sex, slander and profanity. But how explain that Alfonso X, one of the most learned and cultured rulers of thirteenth-century Europe, wrote some of the continent's most obscene lyrics?

Alfonso X (No. 49), Pero da Ponte (No. 22), Joam Airas de Santiago (No. 63) and other Galician-Portuguese troubadours skilfully developed their risqué subjects with rich metaphors, symbols, and a sophisticated range of ironic tones, but the *cantigas d'escarnho* were not all sex and scurrility. Dozens of songs rail against the stinginess (No. 69, No. 70), cowardice (No. 44) or uselessness (No. 24) of rich nobles, against the late or inadequate payment of soldiers (No. 43) and jongleurs (No. 23), against haughty ladies (No. 71) and against incompetent colleagues in the profession (No. 9). Certain *cantigas d'escarnho* have revealed important information about the history, customs and concerns of the time, while the significance of others has remained obscure (No. 42).

In their digs at one another, the Galician-Portuguese poets sometimes resorted to the *tenção* (No. 65, No. 113), which the *Art of Troubadour Poetry* (Section 3, Chapter 7) describes as an exchange of arguments and rebuttals between two troubadours. The treatise states that this mode may occur in all of the major *cantiga* categories, which has led some critics to consider any dialogued *cantiga* (such as between mother and daughter) a *tenção*, but such a loose application of the term violates its basic definition. At most we might consider No. 113 as a *tenção d'amor*, since a troubadour's relation with his lady is in question, though the *cantiga* would be better characterized as one of *escarnho*. The 30 or so *tenções* in the songbooks were mostly composed at Alfonso X's court, which was frequented by such as Pero Garcia d'Ambroa, Pero da Ponte, Joam Garcia de Guilhade, Joam Soarez Coelho, Fernan Garcia Esgaravunha, Gil Perez Conde, Afonso Mendez de Besteiros, Joam Airas de Santiago, Joam Vasquiz de Talaveira, Lourenço, Joam Baveca, Pero Garcia Burgalês, and a steady stream of Provençal troubadours, several of whom also entered the fray, the coterie of poets seeming to have revelled in an orgy of insult. The words of their songs are probably as far as the orgy went, however. Except for the boasts of sexual prowess (No. 12, No. 34), the scandalous events referred to in the *cantigas* no doubt occurred, but they were often blown out of proportion for literary ends. The role of *cantigas* was after all to provide amusement and escape for the rather unamusing life of the courts. And notwithstanding his scathing cantiga against a clergyman fond of pornography (No. 49), Alfonso X was profoundly religious, and probably defended his court against the scandals and licentiousness that so delighted him in poetry.

CANTIGAS EN LOOR DE SANTA MARIA

The 427 *Songs in Praise of Holy Mary* (in fact 9 are repeated and the last 5 praise Jesus) are not usually considered part of the troubadour school, and the *Art of Troubadour Poetry* makes no mention of them. But it was troubadours who composed them, under the direction of Alfonso X, and one of the King's *cantigas* to the Virgin (M 40) can be found in the same Songbook (B 467) that contains the *Troubadour Poetry* treatise. This may well have been due to a mix-up in the King's scriptorium, discussed further on. In fact there were (and are) good reasons not to place the Marian songs under the rubric of troubadour poetry. The hugely different thematic concerns are joined by stylistic differences that are almost as large. Most of the *Cantigas de Santa Maria* (as they came to be known after Alfonso X's death) are narrative, make no use of parallelism or other similar devices, and have a line of up to 22 syllables, with 14 syllables being typical. All but seven of the Marian *cantigas* have refrains, which are likewise found in a majority of the profane *cantigas*, but the predominant stanza type of the former is the virelay, with a rhyme scheme of AAbbba (where AA is the refrain), virtually non-existent in troubadour poetry. The other feature that clearly sets the *Cantigas de Santa Maria* apart is their organic coherence and conceptual unity. The profane Galician-Portuguese Songbooks were, as we shall see, an after-the-fact attempt to impose coherence on a mishmash of short texts, some of which were fragmentary and few of which were conceived with any thought of their contribution to the larger ensemble.

The pet literary project of Alfonso X's later life, the Marian Songbook was successively enlarged, from 100 to 200 to 400 *cantigas*, most of which were composed from 1270 to 1282. As the collection increased, the songs were reordered so as to fit various numerical schemes. At the first doubling, for example, numbers ending in 5 were assigned to the longer songs. In all three versions, the numbers ending in 0 correspond to hymns of praise and/or supplication, with a shorter line and generally fewer stanzas than the narrative songs recounting miracles. And in the final version, the songs whose numbers end in 00 feature the first-person voice of Alfonso X.

Miracles attributed to Mary began to be recorded and collected as early as the sixth century, but it was in the eleventh century that the collections proliferated and assumed large proportions. With the emergence of the preaching orders – the Franciscans in 1209 and the Dominicans in 1216 – religious writings began to appear in vernacular tongues, and major miracle collections were produced in French by Gautier de Coinci (1177-1236), in Spanish by Berceo (c.1195-c.1260) and in Galician-Portuguese by Alfonso X. The first non-Latin collection of Marian miracles, dating from the end of the twelfth century, was written in Anglo-Norman by the London cleric Adgar. The *Cantigas de Santa Maria* was by far the largest of the vernacular collections.

The vastness of the *Cantigas de Santa Maria*, which were written over a relatively short span of time, is itself a sufficient proof that Alfonso X was not their sole author, and for anyone who may still doubt, there is the King's indirect confession, in the first part (Book 16, Chapter 13) of his *General History*: '...the King makes a book, not because he writes it with his hands, but because he composes its arguments, and corrects them, and straightens and perfects them, and shows how they should be made...'. The King referred to is God, who wrote the Scriptures (the text explains) through the hands of his prophets, and nothing would have been more natural than for Alfonso X – as God's earthly representative – to assume the same authorial prerogative. But did he merely oversee the work, or did he actually write some of the texts? A miniature at the beginning of one of the Marian Songbooks (T) shows Alfonso X seated on his throne and flanked by two clerics, one of whom is writing while the other looks up from his parchment to listen. The King is glancing at some open pages and appears to be dictating. To his far left there is a group of four clerics examining a text, and to his far right there is a group of three musicians. Is this an accurate representation of how the songs were composed? Probably not, but it at any rate indicates that a group effort was involved, and the King was part of the group. The name of the Galician cleric Airas Nunez, who was a master troubadour, appears in the most complete manuscript (E) of the *Cantigas de Santa Maria* between the two columns of song 223, and studies have verified certain similarities between his profane *cantigas* (see Nos. 95-97) and many of the Marian songs, so that some scholars believe he may have authored a majority of the *Cantigas de Santa Maria* and/or co-ordinated the group that elaborated them. On the other hand, close to 40 of the Marian songs allude to events in the life of Alfonso X, his family or his court, suggesting that they (and no doubt other songs) depended primarily on his input.

The source material for the more than 350 miracles recounted in the Marian *cantigas* was provided by general miracle collections in Latin (especially Vicente de Beauvais's *Speculum historiale*, compiled in the mid-thirteenth century), by collections associated with specific shrines in France and in Iberia, and by various local oral traditions. Many of the sources, both written and oral, seem to have been gathered by the King on his military expeditions. Besides presenting a rich panorama of both typical and eccentric individuals from various social strata and from various countries, the *Cantigas de Santa Maria* trace an interesting profile of medieval religiosity and moral attitudes. Telling examples are when the Virgin cures a sick monk by giving him milk from her breast (M 54), when she helps two robbers break jail because they promised to contribute nails to a shrine (M 106), and when she refills an empty wine vat for the benefit of drunk pilgrims who wanted to get drunker (M 351).

The Public, the Poets, Manuscripts and Music

Given the central place of the Virgin Mary in the medieval imagination, it would be logical to assume that the *Cantigas de Santa Maria* were destined for the general public, but it seems they never spread very far beyond Alfonso X's court. Tremendous energies were expended to compose and preserve the Marian *cantigas*, but no effort was made to disseminate them. They were a religious poetry for an élite, relying – ironically – on popular sources for their narrative content, and in this respect they may be compared to the *cantigas d'amigo*, whose content as well as form were largely stolen from an oral tradition and reelaborated for the benefit of a restricted, more cultured group of cognoscenti.

If the religious poetry hardly left court, then even less so the profane poetry. A few of the *cantigas d'escarnho* were no doubt made to circulate as propaganda on behalf of certain causes and against certain individuals, but what audience could courtly love poetry have found outside the immediate context that defined it? Troubadour poetry on the Peninsula had a small audience, much smaller than in southern France, where there was a comparatively extensive network of royal and noble courts, and this may explain why the Galician-Portuguese *cantigas* – subject to less critical review – were generally less dazzling than the Provençal *cansos*.

And what of the jongleur who sang in public festivals and on town squares? He and the *jongleresse* existed, working as travelling minstrels or as paid employees of the town council, but they had little to do with court poetry and with those who composed and sang it. In an extensive *Declaratio* to Giraldo Riquier, one of the last Provençal troubadours, Alfonso X[7] distinguished between various categories of composers and performers. *Troubadours*, he stipulated, composed both the lyrics and the melodies of court poetry, and the best among them merited the title of *doctor in the art of troubadour poetry*. (Such a title may have been merited, but it never actually existed.) The court *jongleur* sang what the troubadour composed and was not to be confused with street jongleurs, dubbed *cazuros* [the vile, the vulgar]. Some of the street singers had talent, admitted the King, but they lacked the necessary refinement to be accepted at court, so that it were better to call them *buffoons*, the name applied in Lombardy to those who

---

[7] The *Declaratio* is a long poem in answer to Riquier's even longer *Suplicatio*, both of which were written in the langue d'oc. It was Riquier of course who put words into Alfonso X's mouth, but the two men no doubt discussed the problems of the troubadour's art and professional status during Riquier's sojourn at the Castilian court, and there are other documents revealing the King's concern about such matters. In one of his *cantigas* (B 487/V 70) the King censured Pero da Ponte for not composing like a Provençal poet, and in his *Siete partidas*, a legal code, he banned *cantigas* that calumniated others – this in spite of his own highly slanderous songs.

tamed monkeys, handled marionettes, imitated birds and played the fool.[8]

Some of the court jongleurs worked independently, singing songs of various authors and receiving compensation – usually in the form of food, drink and clothing – from the nobles they entertained. Others were in the employ of a single troubadour, performing his songs and in some cases helping to compose the words or music. Some jongleurs, such as Joam Baveca and Juião Bolseiro, composed their own songs and managed to ascend to the rank of troubadour, but upstarts usually took a lot of abuse from the class-conscious troubadours. Lourenço, a jongleur in the service of Joam Garcia de Guilhade, had to defend himself continually against the insults heaped on him by his master and by other troubadours (No. 65) because of the *cantigas* he composed. Much of the railing was obviously tongue-in-cheek, else the jongleurs' compositions would not have been included in the Songbooks, which were produced in royal scriptoriums.

The Galician-Portuguese troubadours were more often than not of noble lineage, from kings to princes to knights to squires, but some were clerics and others were from the merchant class. All of them were men, so far as we know. (There were a few female troubadours – *trobairitz* – in the Provençal school, including the renowned Beatriz de Dia.) Professional troubadours, according to the *Declaratio*, were known as *segreis* (sing. *segrel*),[9] and it is likely that they also played instruments and sang, being precursors of the court musician of later centuries who would compose and perform as well as teach music to members of the royal house. Troubadouring sometimes ran in the family, so that we find Estevan Coelho following in the footsteps of his troubadour grandfather, Joam Soarez Coelho, and an apprenticeship seems to have been customary for aspiring professionals, as we know from Pero da Ponte, who learned from Afons'Eanes do Coton.

One of the keystones of the classical (and romantic) view of the Middle Ages as a time of intellectual stagnation was the notion that literacy was cloistered within the walls of the monastery. Modern medievalists still

---

[8] All of these activities, along with others not mentioned by the King, such as acrobatics and the magic arts, belonged to the repertoire of the ancient *joculator*, from which the English *jokester* and *juggler* are derived. To speak of the medieval juggler dedicated specifically to music, it is useful to employ the French word *jongleur*.

[9] Much confusion and misunderstanding surrounds this term. See Bertolucci, *La Supplica*, p.35ff. for a thorough examination of the source texts containing it.

concede that physical prowess, fortitude of spirit and moral rectitude were more generally cultivated than the faculty of reason, but historical, philological and archaeological investigations have proven that reading and writing had a fief that ranged over the secular as well as religious terrain, touching not only the upper strata but also the merchant class. It is true that many nobles could read or write little more than their names; it is also true that many humble but free men were functionally literate, a small number of these could pride themselves on being literary, and among these literary there was a small group of musically talented individuals who went on to become troubadours.

A few of the more socially privileged troubadours, such as Osoir'Anes, attended one of the several universities that opened their doors in the twelfth and thirteenth centuries, but the ensemble of troubadours constituted a separate and subversive intellectual force. Not that they actively tried to undermine feudal society, whose noble class supported and sustained them. It was simply that their literary concerns were per se a tremendous provocation. Courtly love was founded on a usurpation and perversion of feudal concepts, and the satiric songs served as an ongoing forum for political and social criticism. The role of the troubadours was in many respects equivalent to the role played by writers in modern society, and it may be actually more accurate to see them as the first modern writers.

But did all of them actually write? If they did not, then someone wrote for them, which amounts to the same thing. A poem may be completely composed in one's mind and recited aloud before it ever reaches paper, or it may be dictated by the author rather than written by his or her own pen, but we would not for these reasons consider the poem an example of oral literature. The mode of transmission is the defining factor, and there are – in addition to historical and theoretical grounds – at least three documentary evidences for supposing that troubadour poetry was transmitted in written form: (1) the various manuscript copies of a given text present one and the same basic version, with variants due almost exclusively to errors in copying or to differing orthographic conventions; (2) the organization of the anthological Songbooks indicates that they were compiled from smaller, often individual songbooks and from loose sheets; and (3) loose sheets with words and music have been found for the work of several troubadours.

There are three fundamental manuscript collections of Galician-Portuguese troubadour poetry.

A The Ajuda Songbook [*Cancioneiro de Ajuda*], discovered in 1759 and presently kept in the library of the Ajuda Palace in Lisbon, is the oldest of the anthological Songbooks. It has many physical characteristics in common with the Marian songbooks and thus was almost surely produced, like these, in the scriptorium of Alfonso X. The complete absence of *cantigas* by King Dinis and other later troubadours confirms this assumption. The Ajuda codex was not completed, and many of its pages were subsequently removed. Space for music was left below the verses of first stanzas, but none of it was written in, and the miniatures were only done in part. The codex does not name the authors of its 310 texts, virtually all of them *cantigas d'amor*, but 246 of the songs can be found in one or both of the other major manuscript collections, in which the authors are identified.

V The Vatican Library Songbook [*Cancioneiro da Vaticana*] was copied in the early sixteenth century by an Italian scribe at the behest of the humanist Angelo Colocci, who penned in the names of the authors and made other occasional notations. No space was left for the music. Discovered in 1840, the Vatican codex contains 1205 *cantigas*.

B The National Library of Lisbon Songbook [*Cancioneiro da Biblioteca Nacional*], known also as the Colocci-Brancuti Songbook, was copied by various hands at about the same time as V and likewise under the sponsorship and direction of Colocci, who transcribed various marginalia with his own hand. No space was left for the music. Discovered in the Brancuti family library in 1878 and ceded to the Portuguese government in 1924, B is the richest source of Galician-Portuguese troubadour poetry, with around 1570 *cantigas*, including all but a few of the texts in V, most of the texts in A, and several hundred texts not found elsewhere. It also includes the *Arte de Trobar*, a fragmentary poetic treatise.

Although there is no consensus among scholars, evidence provided by the recently discovered Sharrer manuscript (see below) tips the scale in favour of the view that V and B were copied from the same manuscript. There is in any event an extremely close relationship between V and B, apparent in the transcriptions and in the order of the *cantigas*, and a less close but indisputable relationship between the two Italian copies and A. To understand how the *cantigas* were transmitted and the major Songbooks compiled, it is useful to consider the following manuscripts, the first two of which are also important for the musical notation that accompanies their text.

R The Vindel Manuscript, named after the Spanish bookseller who discovered it in 1914 in the binding of a fourteenth-century codex, contains seven *cantigas d'amigo* by Martin Codax (Nos. 50-56), with musical notation for all but the sixth. The seven texts appear in the same order as in B and V. Dating almost certainly from the thirteenth century, and thus possibly prepared during the author's lifetime, the manuscript was clearly a loose sheet and not part of a volume. It was acquired by the Pierpont Morgan Library of New York in 1977.

S The Sharrer Manuscript was discovered by Harvey L. Sharrer in 1990, in a bookcover used for a sixteenth-century record of notary documents in Lisbon. Badly mutilated, it contains fragmentary text and musical notation for seven *cantigas d'amor* by King Dinis, and it was probably produced in the King's scriptorium in the early fourteenth century. The manuscript, which is kept at the Portuguese National Archives (Torre do Tombo), is a single folio that belonged to a volume of large proportions. The seven texts appear in the same order in both B and V.

M This seventeenth-century folio, located in the National Library of Madrid, contains a *tenção* by Afonso Sanchez and Vasco Martins de Resende (No. 113), without musical notation. It is a copy of what was probably a loose sheet or roll. The *tenção* is also found in B and V.

P This seventeenth-century folio, located in the Municipal Library of Oporto, contains the same *tenção* as M, without musical notation but with a marginal note indicating that the source text was accompanied by music.

It would be hazardous to draw many conclusions from such meagre manuscript evidence, but it is reasonable to suppose[10] that the *cantigas* originally circulated on loose sheets or rolls for the benefit of the jongleurs who sang them and for the kings and nobles who sponsored the troubadours. Individual songbooks for King Alfonso X and King Dinis almost surely existed, as the inventory of the library of Portugal's King Duarte (1391-1487) mentions both *The Book of Songs of King*

---

[10] The evolution of the Songbooks herein proposed was largely formulated by Giuseppe Tavani. See Chapter 2 of his *A Poesia Lírica* for a fuller discussion of the problems.

Dinis [O Livro das Trovas d'el-Rey D. Diniz] and the *Book of Songs of King Alfonso* [Livro das Trovas d'el-Rey D. Affonso]. It is conceivable that the two monarchs are named in the titles as compilers of anthologies that included various authors, but the placement of their *cantigas* in B and V supports the much more likely hypothesis that each had his own individual songbook. The *cantigas* in B and V are separated into the three main genres – *cantigas d'amor, cantigas d'amigo* and *cantigas d'escarnho* – but Alfonso X's work appears en masse, and is followed by an even larger block of *cantigas* by King Dinis, whose *cantigas d'escarnho* were however removed and placed with others of the same genre at the back of the volume. This division by genres in B and V suggests that there may have been separate songbooks for the *cantigas d'amigo* and the *cantigas d'escarnho*, as there was – in the Ajuda Songbook – for the *cantigas d'amor.*

The manuscript tradition of the *Cantigas de Santa Maria* is much easier to determine, there being four more or less well made and well preserved songbooks, all of them produced in the scriptorium of Alfonso X, and all but F containing musical notation:

To With 127 *cantigas*, the Toledo manuscript (now in the National Library of Madrid) contains the initial, 100-song version of the Marian songbook as well as some additional songs, including 10 not found in E.

T The 193 songs of T, located in the Escorial Library, represent the second version of the *Cantigas de Santa Maria.*

F The Florence Library codex was meant to complement T, after it was decided to redouble the number of songs to 400. F was left incomplete, however, with only 104 of the projected 200 *cantigas*, and the music was not copied in, though space was left for it. F contains 2 songs not found elsewhere.

E Also kept in the Escorial Library, this codex represents the final, complete version of the Marian songbook, with 401 numbered *cantigas*, preceded by 2 introductory *cantigas* and followed by 14 others. There are actually only 408 distinct compositions, nine of which are repeated.

It is interesting to note that among the first 149 folios of T, the only one missing is fol. 40, which contained the same song of praise that appears anomalously, as noted above, amid Alfonso X's troubadour lyrics in B. We can imagine a filing error in Alfonso X's busy scriptorium, the folio having been inadvertently included in a collection of profane *cantigas* authored by the King (or by the King and other troubadours) and then copied and collected into larger, anthological songbooks.

We too often forget that the *cantigas* were songs, many of them no doubt being appreciated for their melodies more than for their words. Unfortunately almost no troubadour lyrics of the Galician-Portuguese school have survived. As noted above, the space intended for music was left blank in the Ajuda Songbook, and there wasn't even space for music in the other two main Songbooks, which were copied several centuries later, when already the musical notation had very likely been lost or was no longer intelligible. The thirteen musically notated *cantigas* discovered in this century have provided models for a very limited number of verse schemes, so that no clear notion of Galician-Portuguese troubadour music has emerged. The Vindel Manuscript's *cantigas d'amigo* by Martin Codax are characterized by a very simple strophic scheme, so that the equally simple melodic scheme gives few clues to the kind of music typical of more structurally complex *cantigas*. The Sharrer Manuscript, on the other hand, presents a comparatively sophisticated melodic line for its seven *cantigas d'amor* by King Dinis, with larger intervals and with more notes per syllable than in the Codax *cantigas*. In these and in other respects, the Sharrer Manuscript confirms that Galician-Portuguese troubadour music followed in the European modal tradition rather than deriving, as some had supposed, from the music of the Moors.

With over 400 melodies assuming many different forms – motets, rondeaus, ballades, etc. – the *Cantigas de Santa Maria* are probably a richer source of medieval music than any other single oeuvre, and its lyrical (more than its narrative) songs can provide keys to understanding the still obscure world of Galician-Portuguese troubadour music. Easy equivalences must of course be avoided; the fact of having the same metrical scheme does not mean that a profane and religious song will have the same melodic structure. But in light of the intimate relationship between the Provençal *canso* and the sacred music contemporary to it, we may at least postulate an analogous relationship between Galician-Portuguese troubadour songs and the *Cantigas de Santa Maria*, particularly since these were composed by troubadours. Should other *cantigas* with musical notation be discovered, then the relations between the various traditions – religious and profane, Peninsular and French, erudite and popular – will become clearer. For the time being, there is among all of the musical texts of the period, whether north or south of the Pyrenees, at least one definite point in common: the rhythms have yet to be determined. Various systems have been proposed in an attempt to make sense of the musical notation where the rhythm is concerned (the melody is not a problem), but timing in the Middle Ages was either a very complicated affair or something that had to be felt rather than determined and that we, outside those Ages, can no longer feel. 'Tempo rubato,' conclude the musicologists in desperation. But I wonder if it isn't more recent ages, including our own, that have robbed time.

RICHARD ZENITH
Lisbon, January 1992

About the Selection and Translation

(1) The 113 *cantigas* of this edition represent a wide variety of types found in the Galician-Portuguese Songbooks, and for that very reason the selection is not proportionately representative. *Cantigas* such as Alfonso X's 'Song of Discomfort' (No. 45), Joam Lobeira's 'Song for Leonorette' (No. 79) and Nun'Eanes Cerzeo's 'Discord' (No. 88) are unique specimens among dozens and dozens of *cantigas* in the Songbooks that repeat a handful of basic formulas.

(2) The English titles are entirely my own invention, and the protesting reader is invited to rub them out. The reason for the titles is to help situate the texts. It can be especially difficult to determine whether a given love song is narrated from a man's or woman's point of view, and while the generic name *Cantiga d'Amor* (from a man's point of view) might be adequately rendered as 'Song of Love', I could not find a satisfactory translation for *Cantiga d'Amigo*. 'Song About a Friend', 'Song About a Lover', 'Song for a Friend [Lover]' and other solutions do not indicate that the narrator is a woman, and 'Girl's Song' is too general in that the subject of the song – love – is unspecified, and not general enough in that the narrator is occasionally the mother (No. 91).

(3) The NOTES TO THE POEMS indicate the original manuscript sources for each *cantiga*, followed by the source for the published version that has been reproduced here. The published versions have been taken from the best editions available, and no attempt has been made to standardize the transcriptions, which obey as many different criteria as there are editors. Punctuation is practically nonexistent in the Songbooks, and the translations pay no special heed to the proposed punctuation of edited versions. The Notes also indicate where the translation has strayed from the original.

(4) The names of the troubadours appear in the Songbooks with as many as four different spellings, and editors often make the spellings conform to the phonetic rules of modern Spanish or Portuguese. I've generally preferred the most oft occurring of the original spellings, with one change and several exceptions: (a) *y* has been regularly replaced by *i*; (b) since 'Johan' would suggest, incorrectly, the German pronunciation for 'Johann', I've used 'Joam', which also appears – less often – in the Songbooks; (c) the names of kings are given according to modern convention.

Acknowledgements

For her general orientation and encouragement: Elsa Gonçalves.

For their help in finding and providing bibliographical material: Elsa Gonçalves, João Dionísio, Ângela Correia, and the library staff of the Centro da Linguística, University of Lisbon.

For their generous financial support: the John Simon Guggenheim Memorial Foundation, the Rockefeller Foundation, and the Instituto de Cultura e Língua Portuguesa.

R.Z.

Bibliography

EDITIONS AND STUDIES

Alvar, Carlos, and Vicente Beltrán. *Antología de la poesía gallego-portuguesa*, Madrid 1985.

Asensio, Eugenio. *Poética y realidad en el cancionero peninsular de la Edad Media*, 2nd edition, Madrid 1970.

Azevedo Filho, Leodegário A. de. *As Cantigas de Pero Meogo*, Rio de Janeiro 1974; 2nd edition, Rio 1981.

Bertolucci-Pizzorusso, Valeria. *Le poesie di Martin Soares*, Bologna 1963.

Blasco, Pierre. *Les chansons de Pero Garcia Burgalês*, Paris 1984.

Cancioneiro da Biblioteca Nacional (Colocci-Brancuti) – Códice 10991, facsimile, intro. Luís F. Lindley Cintra, Lisbon 1982.

Cancioneiro Português da Vaticana (Códice 4803), facsimile, intro. Luís F. Lindley Cintra, Lisbon 1973.

Cunha, Celso Ferreira da. *O Cancioneiro de Joan Zorro*, Rio de Janeiro 1949.

Ferreira, Manuel Pedro. *O Som de Martin Codax*, Lisbon 1986.
— 'Relatório Preliminar sobre o Conteúdo Musical do Fragmento Sharrer' in *Actas do Congresso da Associação Hispânica de Literatura Medieval*, I, Lisbon 1991, pp.35-42.
Gonçalves, Elsa, and Maria Ana Ramos. *A Lírica Galego-Portuguesa*, Lisbon 1985.
Jensen, Frede. *The Earliest Portuguese Lyrics*, Odense 1978.
Lapa, M. Rodrigues. *Cantigas d'escarnho e de mal dizer dos cancioneiros medievais galego-portugueses*, Vigo 1965; revised and enlarged, Vigo 1970.
— *Lições de Literatura Portuguesa*, 10th edition, Coimbra 1981.
— *Miscelânea de Língua e Literatura Portuguesa Medieval*, Coimbra 1982.
Mettmann, Walter, ed. Alfonso X, el Sabio. *Cantigas de Santa Maria*, Coimbra 1959-1972; reprinted, Vigo 1981; revised, Madrid 1986-89.
Michaëlis de Vasconcellos, Carolina. *Cancioneiro da Ajuda*, Halle 1904; reprinted, Lisbon 1990. (Critical Edition of A.)
Monaci, Ernesto, ed. *Il Canzoniere portoghese della Biblioteca Vaticana*, Halle 1875.
Montoya, Jesús, ed. Alfonso X el Sabio. *Cantigas*, Madrid 1988.
Nunes, José Joaquim. *Cantigas de Amigo*, Coimbra 1926-28; reprinted, Lisbon 1973.
— *Cantigas de Amor*, Coimbra 1932; reprinted, Lisbon 1972.
Panunzio, Saverio. *Pero da Ponte. Poesie*, Bari 1967.
Pellegrini, Silvio. *Studi su trove e trovatori della prima lirica ispano-portoghese*, Turin 1937; revised and enlarged, Bari 1959.
Reali, Erilde. 'Il canzoniere di Pedr'Eanes Solaz', in *Annali dell'Istituto Universitario Orientale di Napoli – Sezione Romanza*, IV, Naples 1962, pp.167-195.
— 'Le *cantigas* di Juyão Bolseyro', in *Annali* (ibid.), offprint, Naples 1964.
Reckert, Stephen and Helder Macedo. *Do Cancioneiro de Amigo*, Lisbon 1976.
Rodríguez, José Luis. *El cancionero de Joan Airas de Santiago*, Santiago de Compostela 1980.
Roncaglia, Aurelio. 'Glanures de critique textuelle dans le domaine de l'ancienne lyrique galégo-portugaise: Le *pardon* de la Balteira et le *casamento* de la «tendeira»', in *Actes du colloque international de critique textuelle portugaise (Paris, 20-24 October 1981)*, Paris 1986.
Sharrer, Harvey L. 'Fragmentos de Sete *Cantigas d'Amor* de D.Dinis, Musicadas – uma Descoberta' in *Actas do Congresso da Associação Hispânica de Literatura Medieval*, I, Lisbon 1991, pp.13-29.

Stegagno Picchio, Luciana. *A Lição do Texto*, Lisbon 1979.
— *Martin Moya. Le Poesie*, Rome 1968.
Tavani, Giuseppe. *A Poesia Lírica Galego-Portuguesa*, Lisbon 1990.
— *Le poesie di Ayras Nunez*, Milan 1964.
— *Lourenço. Poesie e tenzoni*, Modena 1964.
— *Poesia del Duecento nella penisola iberica*, Rome 1969.
Toriello, Fernanda. *Fernand'Esquyo. Le Poesie*, Bari 1976.
Vasconcelos, José Leite de. *Textos Arcaicos*, 4th ed., Lisbon 1959.
Zilli, Carmelo. *Johan Baveca. Poesie*, Bari 1977.

ADDITIONAL SOURCES FOR THE INTRODUCTION

Alvar, Carlos. *Textos trovadorescos sobre España y Portugal*, Barcelona 1978.
Ballesteros Berreta, Antonio. *Alfonso X el Sabio*, Barcelona 1963.
Bertolucci-Pizzorusso, Valeria. 'La supplica di Guiraut Riquier e la risposta di Alfonso X di Castiglia' in *Studi mediolatini e volgari*, XIV, Bologna 1966, pp.9-135.
D'Heur, Jean-Marie. *Troubadours d'Oc et troubadours galiciens-portugais*, Paris 1973.
Dronke, Peter. *The Medieval Lyric*, London 1968.
Goff, Jacques Le. *Les intellectuels au Moyen Age*, Paris 1985.
Marrou, Henri-Irénée. *Les troubadours*, Paris 1971.
Mattoso, José. *Identificação de um País*, Lisbon 1988.
Menéndez Pidal, Ramón. *Poesía juglaresca y juglares*, Madrid 1942; 8th edition, 1983.
Riquer, Martín de. *Los trovadores. Historia literaria y textos*, Barcelona 1975; reprinted, 1983.
Saraiva, António José. *A Cultura em Portugal – Teoria e História, Livro II*, Lisbon 1983.
Schaffer, Martha E. 'The Galician-Portuguese Tradition and the Romance *Kharjas*' in *Portuguese Studies*, v.3, London 1987, pp.1-20.
Zumthor, Paul. *La lettre et la voix*, Paris 1987.

113 Galician-Portuguese Troubadour Poems

1 King Sancho I

cantiga d'amigo

Ay eu coitada, como vivo en gran cuidado
por meu amigo que ei alongado!
Muito me tarda
o meu amigo na Guarda!

Ay eu coitada, como vivo en gran desejo
por meu amigo que tarda e não vejo!
Muito me tarda
o meu amigo na Guarda!

1 King Sancho I

Song for a Beloved in Guarda

Ay! what agony,
always longing
for my beloved who's gone!
  How much longer
  will he stay in Guarda?

Ay! what heartache,
always afraid
for my friend who's away!
  How much longer
  will he stay in Guarda?

2 Pai Soarez de Taveirós

cantiga d'amor

Como morreu quen nunca ben
ouve da ren que mais amou,
o quen viu quanto receou
d'ela, e foi morto por én:
    Ay mia senhor, assi moir' eu!

Como morreu quen foi amar
quen lhe nunca quis ben fazer,
e de que[*n*] lhe fez Deus veer
de que foi morto con pesar:
    Ay mia senhor, assi moir' eu!

Com' ome que ensandeceu,
senhor, con gran pesar que viu,
e non foi ledo nen dormiu
depois, mia senhor, e morreu:
    Ay mia senhor, assi moir' eu!

Como morreu quen amou tal
dona que lhe nunca fez ben,
e quen a viu levar a quen
a non valia, nen a val:
    Ay mia senhor, assi moir' eu!

2 Pai Soarez de Taveirós

Song of How I Die

Like one who died because he never
won the woman that he most loved
but saw her do what he most dreaded
and so no longer wished to live,
    that, dear lady, is how I die!

Like one who died for having adored
a woman that never showed him favour
but did, by God, what he most abhorred,
making his life lose all its flavour,
    that, dear lady, is how I die!

Like one, dear lady, who lost his mind
because of the horror that he saw,
and then, unable to sleep or find
any more joy, could not go on,
    that, dear lady, is how I die!

Like one who died for loving a woman
without ever seeing his love returned
and saw her give love to another
by whom it wasn't and isn't deserved,
    that, dear lady, is how I die!

3 Pai Soarez de Taveirós

cantiga d'amor

No mundo non sei parella
mentre me for como me vay,
ca ja moiro por vos e ay!
mia sennor branca/e vermella,
queredes que vus retraya
quando vus eu vj en saya.
Mao dia me leva*n*tey
que vus enton non vi fea!

E, mia señor, des aquel[la]
me foy a mi muy mal di'ay!
E vus, filla de don Paay
Moniz, e ben vus semella
d'aver eu por vos guarvaya,
pois eu, mia señor, d'alfaya
nunca de vos ouve nen ey
valia d'ũa correa.

3 Pai Soarez de Taveirós

Song to a Lady in Simple Clothes

I know of no one else whose plight
can compare to the one I face:
here I am dying for your sake,
and you, dear lady, red and white,
ask for songs with you in robes
when I saw you in simple clothes.
Had I only stayed in bed that day
or found you less well built!

Yes, dear lady, from that day since,
my life has been one big disaster.
What a lot of nerve you have,
daughter of Pai Moniz, to think
that I should put you in fine robes
when from you, in terms of clothes,
I've never had, beloved lady,
so much as a lousy belt.

4 Gil Sanchez

cantiga d'amor

Tu, que ora vẽes de Monte-mayor,
Tu que ora vẽes de Monte-mayor,
digas-me mandado de mia senhor;
digas-me mandado de mia senhor,
ca se eu seu mandado
non vir', trist' e coitado
serei; e gran pecado
fará, se me non val.
Ca en tal ora nado
foi que ¡mao-pecado!
amo-a endõado,
e nunca end' òuvi al!

Tu, que ora viste os olhos seus,
Tu, que ora viste os olhos seus,
digas-me mandado d'ela, por Deus;
digas-me mandado d'ela, por Deus,
ca se eu seu mandado
non vir', trist' e coitado
serei; e gran pecado
fará, se me non val.
Ca en tal ora nado
foi que ¡mao-pecado!
amo-a endõado,
e nunca end' òuvi al!

4 Gil Sanchez

Song for a Word from Monte-Maior

You who from Monte-Maior have come,
you who from Monte-Maior have come,
give me a word from the lady I love,
give me a word from the lady I love,
    for if she hasn't sent
    me word, she will have rent
    my heart, and what regret
    I'll feel, and how slighted,
    for I was born on a day
    that made my heart condemned
    to loving without an end –
    alas! she's never requited.

You who've just now seen her eyes,
you who've just now seen her eyes,
give me a word, by God on high,
give me a word, by God on high,
    for if she hasn't sent
    me word, she will have rent
    my heart, and what regret
    I'll feel, and how slighted,
    for I was born on a day
    that made my heart condemned
    to loving without an end –
    alas! she's never requited.

5 Osoir'Anes

cantiga d'amor

Cuidei eu de meu coraçon
que me non podesse forçar
(pois me sacara de prison)
de ir comego i tornar!
E forçou-m' ora nov' amor,
e forçou-me nova senhor;
e cuido ca me quer matar.

E pois m(e) assi desemparar
ũa senhor foi, des enton
e[*u*] cuidei ben per ren que non
podesse mais outra cobrar.
Mais forçaron-mi os olhos meus
e o bon parecer dos seus,
e o seu preç', e un cantar,

Que lh' oí, u a vi estar
en cabelos, dizend' un son.
¡Mal-dia non morri enton,
ante que tal coita levar,
qual levo! que non vi mayor
nunca, ond' estou a pavor
de mort[*e*], ou de lh'o mostrar.

5 Osoir'Anes

Song of a Man Gone Back to Prison

I never thought that my heart
would be able to force me back
into the prison of passion
I had only lately departed.
It forced on me a new love
and forced on me a new lady,
I guess to make me a martyr!

Having once suffered the loss
of a lady I greatly loved,
I thought I could never be touched
by others who happened along,
but I've been forced by my eyes
and the beauty in hers that shine,
and her worthiness and a song

I heard her sing when her hair
was uncovered. O fateful day!
I wish I'd been given death
instead of having to bear
this pain in my heart, severe
to the point I sincerely fear
I must die or my love declare.

6 Fernan Rodriguez de Calheiros

cantiga d'amigo

Madre, passou per aqui un cavaleiro
e leixou-me namorad' e com marteiro:
ai, madre, os seus amores ei;
se me los ei,
ca mi-os busquei,
outros me lhe dei;
ai, madre, os seus amores ei.

Madre, passou per aqui un filho d'algo
e leixou-m'assi penada, com'eu ando:
ai, madre, os seus amores ei;
se me los ei,
ca mi-os busquei,
outros me lhe dei;
ai, madre, os seus amores ei.

Madre, passou per aqui quen non passasse
e leixou-m'assi penada, mais leixasse:
ai, madre, os seus amores ei;
se me los ei,
ca mi-os busquei,
outros me lhe dei;
ai, madr', os seus amores ei.

6 Fernan Rodriguez de Calheiros

Song of a Girl Who Sought Love

Mother, it was here that I met a young lord
who left me with love and a martyr's torment.
  Ah, mother, how I'm in love!
    If I'm in love it's
    because I sought it,
    but he also caught it.
  Ah, mother, how I'm in love!

Mother, it was here I met a young noble,
who left me with the grief you've noticed.
  Ah, mother, how I'm in love!
    If I'm in love it's
    because I sought it,
    but he also caught it.
  Ah, mother, how I'm in love!

Mother, it was here – had it only not been! –
that he left me grieving – oh, let it be!
  Ah, mother, how I'm in love!
    If I'm in love it's
    because I sought it,
    but he also caught it.
  Ah, mother, how I'm in love!

7 Fernan Rodriguez de Calheiros

cantiga d'amigo

Que farei agor', amigo?
pois que non queredes migo
viver,
ca non poss'eu al ben querer.

En gran coita me leixades,
se vós alhur ir cuidades
viver,
ca non poss'eu al ben querer.

Se aquesta ida vossa
fôr, non sei eu como possa
viver,
ca non poss'eu al ben querer,

Matar-m'ei, se mi-o dizedes
que vós ren sen mi podedes
viver,
ca non poss'eu al ben querer.

7 Fernan Rodriguez de Calheiros

Song to a Beloved Who's Going Away

And what, friend, will I do
if with me you refuse
    to live?
For you are all I want in life.

You'll cause me great distress
if you go anywhere else
    to live,
for you are all I want in life.

If you make this journey,
I'll have no more reason
    to live,
for you are all I want in life.

Kill myself is what I'll do
if without me you
    can live,
for you are all I want in life.

8 Lopo

cantiga d'amigo

– Filha, se gradoedes,
dizede que avedes.
– Non mi dan amores vagar.

– Filha, se ben ajades,
dizede, non mençades.
– Non mi dan amores vagar.

– Dizede, pois vos mando,
por que ides chorando.
– Non mi dan amores vagar.

– Par San Leuter vos digo:
cuidand'en meu amigo,
– Non mi dan amores vagar.

8 Lopo

Song of a Restless Heart

Daughter, if you please,
tell me why you grieve.
  My heart is all unrest.

Daughter, if you would,
tell the honest truth.
  My heart is all unrest.

Give a straight reply!
Why is it you're crying?
  My heart is all unrest.

I swear by St Eleutherius:
thinking about my lover,
  my heart is all unrest.

9 Martin Soarez

cantiga d'escarnho

Foy hun dia Lopo jograr
a cas d'um infançon cantar
e mandou-lh'ele por don dar
tres couces na guarganta;
e fuy-lh'escass'a meu cuydar,
    segundo com'el canta.

Escasso foy o infançon
en sseus couces partir ento*n*,
ca non deu a Lop[o] enton
mays de tres na guarga*n*ta;
e mays m*er*ece/ o jograron,
    segundo com'el canta.

9 Martin Soarez

Song about Lopo the Jongleur

Lopo the jongleur one day went
to sing at the house of a nobleman,
who promptly ordered that Lopo get
three swift kicks below his chin,
which was too lenient in my opinion,
judging by the way he sings.

The nobleman was much too lenient
in the number of kicks he ordered,
for Lopo was only inconvenienced
with three of them below his chin;
that joke of a jongleur deserved more,
judging by the way he sings.

10 Martin Soarez

cantiga d'amor

Senhor fremosa, poys me non queredes
creer a coyta'n que me ten Amor,
por meu mal é que tan ben parecedes
e por meu mal vus filhey por senhor,
e por meu mal tan muyto ben oý
dizer de vos, e por meu mal vus vj:
poys meu mal é quanto ben vos avedes.

E pois v*us* vos da coita no*n* ne*n*brades
nen do affam q*ue* mh-o/ Amor faz sofrer,
por meu mal vyvo mays ca vos cuydades,
e por meu mal me fezo D*eu*s nacer
e por meu mal no*n* morri hu cuidey
como v*us* viss', e por meu mal fiq*ue*i
vivo, poys vos por meu mal ren no*n* dades.

D'esta coyta en que me vos tẽedes,
en que oj'eu vivo tan sen sabor,
q*ue* farei eu, pois mi-a vos no*n* creedes?
Q*ue* farey eu, cativo pecador,
Q*ue* farei eu, vive*n*do sempre /assy?
Q*ue* farei eu, q*ue* mal dia naci?
Q*ue* farei eu, poys me vos no*n* valedes,

E poys que Deus non q*ue*r q*ue* me valhades
nem me q*ue*irades mha coita creer,
q*ue* farey eu? Por D*eu*s, q*ue* mh-o digades!
Q*ue* farei eu, se logo no*n* morrer?
Q*ue* farei eu se mays a viver ey?
Q*ue* farey eu, q*ue* consselh'i no*n* ey?
Q*ue* farey eu, q*ue* vos desenparades?

Song to an Unbelieving Lady

Dear lady, since you refuse to believe
how I grieve out of love for you,
know it's my curse that you're so beautiful,
and it's my curse that I chose you,
and it's my curse that I heard of your fame,
and it's my curse that I saw your face,
for my curse consists in your every grace.

Since you completely ignore my grief
and the fact that for you my heart is torn,
know that my curse is worse than you think,
and it's my curse to have been born,
and it's my curse that I didn't die
the day I saw you and a curse that I
still live, since to my curse you're blind.

Thanks to you I suffer this grief
that makes me live without any pleasure.
What will I do, since you don't believe me?
What will I do, such a miserable wretch?
What will I do living life in this way?
What will I do, regretting each birthday?
What will I do against your disdain?

And since God doesn't want you to help me,
and you don't want to believe I'm grieving,
what will I do? For God's sake, tell me!
What will I do if I keep on living?
What will I do if I don't die soon?
What will I do? There's no solution!
What will I do, denied by you?

11 Afons'Eanes do Coton

cantiga d'escarnho

Abadessa, oí dizer
que érades mui sabedor
de todo ben; e, por amor
de Deus, querede-vos doer
de min, que ogano casei,
que ben vos juro que non sei
mais que un asno de foder.

Ca me fazen en sabedor
de vós que avedes bon sen
de foder e de todo ben;
ensinade-me mais, senhor,
como foda, ca o non sei,
nen padre nen madre non ei
que m' ensin', e fiqu' i pastor.

E se eu ensinado vou
de vós, senhor, deste mester
de foder e foder souber
per vós, que me Deus aparou,
cada que per foder, direi
Pater Noster e enmentarei
a alma de quen m' ensinou.

E per i podedes gaar,
mia senhor, o reino de Deus:
per ensinar os pobres seus
mais ca por outro jajũar,
e per ensinar a molher
coitada, que a vós veer,
senhor, que non souber ambrar.

11 Afons'Eanes do Coton

Song to a Learned Abbess

Dear abbess, I have heard
that you are very learned
about what's good; for love
of God, please have mercy
on me, as I know nothing
more than an ass about fucking
and just this year got married.

I've heard that when it comes
to fucking and other good fun
you're very well informed,
so teach me how to fuck,
Madam, as I'm untrained:
my parents never explained,
and I remained quite dumb.

And if by you I'm told
about the art of screwing,
and if I learn to do it
from you in your Godly role
as abbess, each time I fuck
I'll say a solemn *Our Father*,
and I'll say it for your soul.

I'm certain, Madam, that you
can thus attain God's kingdom:
by teaching all your sinners
more than abstaining from food,
and especially by teaching women
who come to seek your wisdom
about how they should screw.

12 Afons'Eanes do Coton

cantiga d'escarnho

Marinha, en tanto folegares
tenho eu por desaguisado;
e sõo mui maravilhado
de ti, por non [ar]rebentares:
ca che tapo eu [d]aquesta minha
boca a ta boca, Marinha;
e con estes narizes meus
tapo eu, Marinha, os teus;
e co'as mãos as orelhas,
os olhos e as sobrencelhas;
tapo-t' ao primeiro sono
da mia pissa o teu cono,
como me non vej' a nengũu,
e dos colhões esse cuu.
Como non rebentas, Marinha?

12 Afons'Eanes do Coton

Song to an Unexploding Woman

Just look at my confounded state –
Marinha, how you fornicate!
I am really quite astounded
that you haven't yet exploded,
  for with my mouth I cover
  your mouth completely over,
  and with my nose I close
  the nostrils of your own,
  and with my hands I hide
  your ears and brows and eyes,
  and as the first sleep comes
  my cock fills up your cunt,
  and my balls your arse
  – no man has my art!
How do you not explode, Marinha?

13 Pero Garcia d'Ambroa

cantiga d'escarnho

Pedi eu o cono a ũa molher,
e pediu-m' ela cen soldos enton;
e dixe-lh' eu logo: – Mui sen razon
me demandades; mais, se vos prouguer,
fazed' ora – e faredes melhor –
ũa soldada polo meu amor
a de parte, ca non ei mais mester.

Fazen soldada do ouro, que val
mui mais ca o vosso cono, de pran;
fazen soldada de ver[ça], de pan,
fazen soldada de carn' e de sal;
poren devedes do cono fazer
soldada, ca non á de falescer,
se retalhardes, quen vos compr' o al.

E podede-lo vender – eu o sei –
tod' a retalho, por que saberan
que retalhades, e comprar-vos-an
todos d' el parte, como eu comprei.
Ainda vos d' al farei mui melhor:
se do embiigo avedes sabor,
contra o rabo vo-lo filharei.

13 Pero Garcia d'Ambroa

Song about a Woman Who Charged Too Much

I asked a woman for her cunt,
she quoted me a high price,
and so I said: 'You have no right
to charge me such an outrageous sum.
Now do me and yourself a favour –
sell me a portion of your wares,
as my love won't require much.

'Merchants sell small portions of gold,
worth more than your cunt, you will agree.
They sell small portions of bread and greens;
for meat and salt, the same thing holds.
Thus you too should sell your cunt,
for someone will eventually come
and buy the portions you haven't sold.

'And you'd be able – if you're smart –
to sell it all, for word would spread
that you sell piecemeal, and many men
like me would willingly buy a part.
And I'll yet show you a special favour:
if you want to keep your navel,
I'll be happy to take your arse.'

14 Pero Gomez Barroso

sirventês

Do que sabia nulha rén non sei,
polo mundo, que vej' assi andar;
e, quand' i cuido, ei log' a cuidar,
per boa fé, o que nunca cuidei:
    ca vej' agora o que nunca vi
    e ouço cousas que nunca oí.

Aqueste mundo, par Deus, non é tal
qual eu vi outro, non á gran sazon;
e por aquesto, no meu coraçon,
aquel desej' e este quero mal,
    ca vej' agora o que nunca vi
    e ouço cousas que nunca oí.

E non receo mia morte poren,
e, Deus lo sabe, queria morrer,
ca non vejo de que aja prazer
nen sei amigo de que diga ben:
    ca vej' agora o que nunca vi
    e ouço cousas que nunca oí.

E, se me a min Deus quisess' atender,
per boa fé, ũa pouca razon,
eu post' avia no meu coraçon
de nunca já mais neun ben fazer,
    ca vej' agora o que nunca vi
    e ouço cousas que nunca oí.

E non daria ren por viver i
en este mundo mais do que vivi.

14 Pero Gomez Barroso

Song about a Worsening World

Things I knew I know no longer
in this world that's changed so much,
and thinking about it I find I must
think in ways I never thought,
    for I'm seeing things I've never seen
    and hearing things I've never heard.

This world, God knows, is not the same
as what I remember from my youth,
and could I choose between the two,
I'd take the old one any day,
    for I'm seeing things I've never seen
    and hearing things I've never heard.

I have no reason to fear death,
and in fact I'd like to die,
as there's no pleasure in this life
and no one I can call my friend,
    for I'm seeing things I've never seen
    and hearing things I've never heard.

I hope and pray God will accept
the way I think for my own part,
as I've decided in my heart
never to do good works again,
    for I'm seeing things I've never seen
    and hearing things I've never heard.

And I wouldn't give two cents to live
any longer here than what I've lived.

15 Pero Mafaldo

sirventês

Vej' eu as gentes andar revolvendo,
e mudando aginha os corações
do que põen antre si as nações;
e já m' eu aquesto vou aprendendo
e ora cedo mais aprenderei:
a quen poser preito, mentir-lho-ei.
e assi irei melhor guarecendo.

Ca vej' eu ir melhor ao mentireiro
c' ao que diz verdade ao seu amigo;
e por aquesto o jur' e o digo
que já mais nunca seja verdadeiro;
mais mentirei e firmarei log' al:
a quen quero [i] ben, querrei-lhe mal,
e assi guarrei come cavaleiro.

Pois que meu prez nen mia onra non crece,
por que me quígi teer à verdade,
vede-lo que farei, par car[i]dade,
pois que vej' o que m' assi acaece:
mentirei ao amigo e ao senhor,
e poiará meu prez e meu valor
con mentira, pois con verdade dece.

15 Pero Mafaldo

Song on How to Win Fame and Honour

I've seen how people are overturning
all the mores they had established
within their various social classes,
and now I too am finally learning
(and learning faster every day)
to lie in every oath I make
until at last my luck starts turning.

I see that it's the liar who thrives
rather than an honest friend,
and so I swear never again
to say what's really on my mind.
I'll lie point-blank and that's not all:
those that I love I'll now defraud,
thereby prospering like a knight.

I've never known much honour or fame
because I've always stuck to truth,
so here is what I'm going to do
to make the situation change:
I'll lie to God and to my friend
so as to boost my honour and fame,
since by truth they only waned.

16 Pero Gonçalves de Porto Carreiro

cantiga d'amigo

Par Deus, coitada vivo:
pois non ven meu amigo:
pois non vem, que farei?
meus cabelos, con sirgo
eu non vos liarei.

Pois non ven de Castela,
non é viv', ai mesela,
ou mi-o detem el-rei:
mias toucas da Estela,
eu non vos tragerei.

Pero m'eu leda semelho,
non me sei dar conselho;
amigas, que farei?
en vós, ai meu espelho,
eu non me veerei.

Estas dõas mui belas
el mi-as deu, ai donzelas,
non vo-las negarei:
mias cintas das fivelas,
eu non vos cingerei.

16 Pero Gonçalvez de Porto Carreiro

Song for an Unreturned Lover

How grieved is my heart,
for my lover's not here,
and now what will I do?
        O ribbon for my hair,
        you will never be used.

He's still in Castile,
either dead – it can't be! –
or detained by the court.
        O bonnets he gave me,
        you will never be worn.

I may seem content,
but I'm really upset,
so now what, dear sisters?
        I'll gaze at myself
        no more, O mirror.

The beautiful presents
he bought me, dear friends,
I cannot forsake.
        O gold-buckled belts,
        you won't touch my waist.

17 Nuno Fernandez Torneol

cantiga d'amigo

Levad', amigo que dormides as manhanas frias;
todalas aves do mundo d'amor dizian.
Leda mh and'eu.

Levad', amigo que dormide-las frias manhanas;
todalas aves do mundo d'amor cantavan.
Leda m'and'eu.

Todalas aves do mundo d'amor dizian:
do meu amor e do voss'en ment'avyan.
Leda [m'and'eu].

Todalas aves do mundo d'amor cantavan:
do meu amor e do voss'y enmentavan.
Leda [m'and'eu].

Do meu amor e do voss'en ment'avyan;
vós lhi tolhestes os ramus en que siian.
Leda [m'and'eu].

Do meu amor e do voss'y enmentavan;
vós lhi tolhestes os ramus en que pousavan.
Leda [m'and'eu].

Vós lhi tolhestes os ramus en que siian
e lhis secastes as fontes en que bevian.
Leda [m'and'eu].

Vós lhi tolhestes os ramus en que pousavan
e lhis secastes as fontes hu sse banhavan.
Leda [m'and'eu].

17 Nuno Fernandez Torneol

Song for a Sleeping Lover

Rise up, beloved, who on cold mornings sleeps;
all the birds of the world proclaimed love –
 I'm a happy soul.

Rise up, beloved, who on clear mornings sleeps;
all the birds of the world sang love –
 I'm a happy soul.

All the birds of the world proclaimed love;
they had my love and yours in mind –
 I'm a happy soul.

All the birds of the world sang love;
their songs proclaimed my love and yours –
 I'm a happy soul.

They had my love and yours in mind;
you pulled them from their branches –
 I'm a happy soul.

Their songs proclaimed my love and yours;
you pulled them away from where they perched –
 I'm a happy soul.

You pulled them from their branches;
you dried the fountains where they drank –
 I'm a happy soul.

You pulled them away from where they perched;
you dried the fountains where they basked –
 I'm a happy soul.

18 Nuno Fernandez Torneol

cantiga d'amigo

Vi eu, mia madr', andar
as barcas eno mar:
e moiro-me d'amor.

Foi eu, madre, veer
as barcas eno ler:
e moiro-me d'amor.

As barcas [e]no mar
e foi-las aguardar:
e moiro-me d'amor.

As barcas eno ler
e foi-las atender:
e moiro-me d'amor.

E foi-las aguardar
e non o pud' achar:
e moiro-me d'amor.

E foi-las atender
e non o pudi veer:
e moiro-me d'amor.

E non o achei i,
[o] que por meu mal vi:
e moiro-me d'amor.

18 Nuno Fernandez Torneol

Song for an Unreturned Sailor

Mother, I have seen
the ships in from sea,
  and I'm dying of love.

Mother, I watched as
the ships weighed in,
  and I'm dying of love.

The ships in from sea,
I went to meet them,
  and I'm dying of love.

The ships weighed in,
I went and I waited,
  and I'm dying of love.

I went to meet them
but I could not see him,
  and I'm dying of love.

I went and I waited
but could not locate him,
  and I'm dying of love.

I could not see him
who caused me this grieving,
  and I'm dying of love.

19 Pedr'Eanes Solaz

cantiga d'amigo

Eu, velida, non dormia,
lelia doura,
e meu amigo venia,
edoy lelia doura!

Non dormia e cuydava,
lelia doura,
e meu amigo chegava,
edoy lelia doura!

O meu amigo venia,
lelia doura,
e d'amor tan ben dizia,
edoy lelia doura!

O meu amigo chegava,
lelia doura,
e d'amor tan ben cantava,
edoy lelia doura!

Muyto desejey amigo,
lelia doura,
que vós tevesse comigo,
edoy lelia doura!

Muyto desejey amado,
lelia doura,
que vós tevesse ao meu lado,
edoy lelia doura!

Lely, lely, par Deus, lely,
lelia doura,
ben sei eu quen non diz lely,
edoy lelia doura!

19 Pedr'Eanes Solaz

Song for a Sleepless Night

I sit up and wonder,
   dellaly dare,
if you're still coming,
   way dellaly dare.

I sit up all night,
   dellaly dare,
until you arrive,
   way dellaly dare.

When finally you come,
   dellaly dare,
you sing words of love,
   way dellaly dare.

When at last you arrive,
   dellaly dare,
you lull me with rhymes,
   way dellaly dare.

How long I've been wishing,
   dellaly dare,
to have you here with me,
   way dellaly dare.

How long I've desired you
   dellaly dare,
here by my side and
   way dellaly dare.

Dell dell, by God, dell
   dellaly dare,
who doesn't dell
   way dellaly dare?

Ben sey eu quen non diz lely,
lelia doura,
demo x'é quen non diz lelia,
edoy lelia doura!

I'll tell who doesn't dell,
  dellaly dare:
the devil never dells
  way dellaly dare.

20 Pero da Ponte

cantiga d'amor

Senhor do corpo delgado,
en forte pont'eu fuy nado!
Que nunca perdi coydado
nen afan, des que vus vi.
En forte pont'eu fui nado,
senhor, por vos e por mi!

Con est'affan tan longado,
en forte pont'eu fui nado!
Que vus amo sen meu grado
e faç'a vos pesar hy.
En forte pont'eu fui nado,
senhor, por vos e por mi!

Ay eu, cativ'e coitado,
en forte pont'eu fui nado!
Que servi sempr'endonado
ond'un ben nunca prendi.
En forte pont'eu fui nado,
senhor, por vos e por mi!

20 Pero da Ponte

Song about a Bad Day

Dear lady, loveliest of ladies,
I was born on a bad day,
for ever since I saw your face
my life's been constant pain and worry.
I was born on a bad day,
lady, for you and for me!

Being condemned to this pain so great,
I was born on a bad day.
To love you is my hateful fate,
and I know my love makes you displeased.
I was born on a bad day,
lady, for you and for me!

I lead a life no better than death.
I was born on a bad day
to serve in vain a lovely dame
from whom I never got a thing.
I was born on a bad day,
lady, for you and for me!

21 Pero da Ponte

cantiga d'amor

Se eu podesse desamar
a quen me sempre desamou,
e podess'algun mal buscar
a quen mi sempre mal buscou!
Assy me vingaria eu,
  se eu podesse coyta dar,
  a quen mi sempre coyta deu.

Mays sol non posso eu enganar
meu coraçon que m'enganou,
per quanto mi faz desejar
a quen me nunca desejou.
E per esto non dormio eu,
  porque non poss'eu coita dar,
  a quen mi sempre coyta deu.

Mays rog'a Deus que desampar
a quen mh'assy desamparou,
ou que podess'eu destorvar
a quen me sempre destorvou.
E logo dormiria eu,
  se eu podesse coyta dar,
  a quen mi sempre coyta deu.

Vel que ousass'en preguntar
a quen me nunca preguntou,
per que me fez en ssy cuydar,
poys ela nunca en min cuydou.
E por esto lazero eu,
  porque non poss'eu coyta dar,
  a quen mi sempre coyta deu.

21 Pero da Ponte

Song of a Lover Who Would Hate

If I could only learn to hate
the one who's always hated me!
If I could only make her hurt
for all the ways that she's hurt me!
I would have revenge at least
    if I could pay back part of the grief
    to the heart that so grieved me.

But I can't even learn to fool
my very own heart – it fooled me
by making me completely fall
for one who'd never fall for me.
And this is why I never sleep:
    I try but can't return the grief
    to the heart that so grieved me.

I pray that God will yet reject
the one who always rejected me,
or that I'll make her feel upset
for all the times she upset me.
I think I'd finally sleep in peace
    if I could pay back part of the grief
    to the heart that so grieved me.

Or that I'll bring myself to ask
the one too cold to ever ask me,
why I've always thought of her,
though she's never thought of me!
And this is why my song is grim:
    I try but can't return the grief
    to the heart that so grieved me.

22 Pero da Ponte

cantiga d'escarnho

Maria Pérez, a nossa cruzada,
quando veo da terra d'Ultramar,
assy veo de pardon carregada,
que se non podia con ele merger;
mays furtan-lh'o, cada hu vay maer,
e do perdon ja non lhi ficou nada.

E o perdon é cousa mui preçada,
e que sse devya muyt'aguardar;
mays ela non á maeta ferrada
en que o guarde, nen a pod'aver:
ca, poys o cadead'en foy perder,
sempr'a maeta andou descadeada.

Tal maeta como será guardada,
poys rapazes albergan no logar,
que non aja seer mui trastornada?
Ca, o logar hu eles an poder,
non á pardon que ss'y possa asconder:
¡assy saben trastornar a pousada!

E outra cousa vus quero dizer:
tal perdon ben sse devera perder,
ca muyto foy [el] cousa mal gaada.

22 Pero da Ponte

Song about a Lost Crusade

On her return from the Holy Land
Maria Perez, our crusaderess,
was carrying so many indulgences
that she couldn't possibly sink,
but they were filched along the way
until not a single one remained.

Indulgences are a precious thing,
to be kept under lock and key,
but she didn't have a decent box
with a lock in which to keep them,
for ever since the lock was broken
her box has been left open.

How can a box like that be safe
in lodgings full of young men
who are bound to go all through it?
For in every place where they prevail
there's no indulgence that won't be found:
they'll turn the hospice upside down!

There's one more thing I should point out:
the indulgences deserved to be lost,
being as they weren't very honestly got.

23 Pero da Ponte

cantiga d'escarnho

Garcia Lopez d'Elfaro,
direy-vus que m'agravece
que vosso don é mui caro:
e vosso don é rafece!
O vosso don é mui caro pera quen o á d'aver,
o vosso don é rafec[e] a quen o á de vender.

Por carus teemus panus
que home pedir non ousa;
e, poy'lus tragen dous anus,
rafeces son per tal cousa.
O vosso don é mui caro pera quen o á d'aver,
o vosso don é rafece a quen o á de vender.

Esto nunca eu cuydara:
que huna cousa senlheira
podesse seer [mui] cara
e rafez'en tal maneyra.
O vosso don é mui caro pera quen o á d'aver,
o vosso don é rafece a quen o á de vender.

23 Pero da Ponte

Song about Costly Cheap Goods

Garcia Lopez del Faro,
I'll tell you why I'm piqued:
the things you give are costly
and at the same time cheap.
Your gifts are costly to obtain,
but cheap if one then tries to sell them.

It costs a lot of labour
to earn your gift of cloths,
but since they're two years old,
they're cheap: they're full of moths.
Your gifts are costly to obtain,
but cheap if one then tries to sell them.

I never thought it possible
that one and the same thing
could be so very costly
and so extremely cheap.
Your gifts are costly to obtain,
but cheap if one then tries to sell them.

24 Pero da Ponte

cantiga d'escarnho

En almoeda vi estar
oj'un ricom'e diss'assy:
– Quen quer hun ricome comprar? –
E nunca hy comprador vi
que o quisesse nen en don;
ca dizian todus que non
daria hun soldo por ssy.

E d'este ricome quen quer
vus pode a verdade dizer:
poys non aprês nen hun mester,
quen querrá hi o seu perder?
Ca el non faz nen hun lavor
de que nulh'om'aja sabor,
nen sab'adubar de comer.

E, hu foron po-lo vender,
preguntaron-o en gran sen:
– Ricom', que sabedes fazer? –
E o ricome disse: – Ren!
Non amo custa nen misson,
mays compro mui de coraçon
erdade, se mh'a vend'alguen –.

E poys el diss'esta razon,
non ouv'i molher nen baron
que por el dar quisesse ren.

24 Pero da Ponte

Song about a Rich Man Up for Auction

I saw a rich man being auctioned
by a dealer who called out loud,
'What do I hear for a rich man?',
but not a buyer could be found
who wanted him at any price.
'For that man there,' they all cried,
'we wouldn't put a nickel down.'

Anyone there could tell you why
the task of the auctioneer was futile:
the rich man never learned a trade,
and who would pay for a useless fool?
He doesn't do any kind of work
that might to a buyer be of worth,
nor can he fix the simplest food.

When they put him up for sale,
indeed they asked the man himself,
'Well, rich man, what can you do?'
'Nothing at all,' the rich man said:
'I hate to work and hate to spend,
although I do like buying land,
if you have any you'd like to sell.'

After they had heard all this,
not one man or woman present
offered even the slightest pittance.

25 Pero da Ponte

cantiga d'escarnho

'Esta cantiga fez Pero da Ponte
ao ynfante don Manuel que se começa:
é morto do[n] M[artin] Marcos, et na cobra
segonda o poden de entender'.

Mort'é don Martin Marcus! Ay Deus, se é verdade!
Sey ca, se el é morto, morta é torpidade,
morta é bavequya e morta neyciidade,
morta é covardia e morta é maldade.
Se don Martinh'é morto, sen prez e sen bondade,
ôy mays, maos costumes, outro senhor catade;
mays nono acharedes de Roma atá cidade:
se tal senhor queredes, alhu'-lo demandade.

Pero hun cavaleyro sey eu, par caridade,
que vus ajudari'a tolher d'el soydade;
mays [per] que vus [eu] diga ende ben [a] verdade:
non est rey, nen conde, mays é-x'outra podestade,
que [vus eu] non direy, que direy, que non direy...

25 Pero da Ponte

Song about a Dead and Living Ass

This song by Pero da Ponte, dedicated to the infante Don Manuel begins 'Martin Marcus is dead!', and you'll see the connection in the second stanza.

Martin Marcus is dead! God grant it may be!
For if he is dead, it's death to stupidity,
death to folly and death to dull-headedness,
death to cowardice and death to ineptness.
If Martin is dead, then listen, Bad Habits,
you'll have to go look for another dumb ass,
but as there's no equal between here and Rome,
you'll have to go look on some other road.

Now I do know of a man, it just so happens,
who could probably cure you of your nostalgia,
and I hope you'll see who I have in mind:
not a king or a count but of a noble line
that I can't say, I'm saying, can't say…

26 Joam Garcia de Guilhade

cantiga d'amor

Amigos, non poss' eu negar
a gran coita que d'amor ei,
ca me vejo sandeu andar,
e con sandece o direi:
Os olhos verdes que eu vi
me fazen or(a) andar assi.

Pero quen-quer x'entenderá
aquestes olhos quaes son;
e d'est' alguen se queixará;
mais eu, ja quer moira, quer non:
Os olhos verdes que eu vi
me fazen or(a) andar assi.

Pero non devi' a perder
ome, que ja o sen non á,
de con sandece ren dizer;
e con sandece digu' eu ja:
Os olhos verdes que eu vi
me fazen or(a) andar assi.

26 Joam Garcia de Guilhade

Song of the Green Eyes

I cannot hide from you, my friends,
how very badly love has hit me,
for you can see how mad I act,
and quite madly I'll admit it:
  the green eyes that I saw
  have made me what you see.

Though everyone knows exactly whom
these eyes belong to, and though the who
I'm speaking of resents the fact,
I'm dying of love – what can I do?
  The green eyes that I saw
  have made me what you see.

If a man has lost his mind,
then he has nothing left to lose
saying mad things in his mad way,
and so I madly say to you:
  the green eyes that I saw
  have made me what you see.

27 Joam Garcia de Guilhade

cantiga d'amigo

Vistes, mias donas, quando noutro dia
o meu amigo comigo falou,
foi mui queixos'e, pero se queixou,
dei-lh'eu enton a cinta que tragia,
mais el demanda-m'[or'] outra folia.

E vistes (que nunca, nunca tal visse!)
por s'ir queixar, mias donas, tan sen guisa,
fez-mi tirar a corda da camisa
e dei-lh'eu d'ela ben quanta m'el disse,
mais el demanda-mi al, que non pedisse.

Sempr'[a]verá don Joan de Guilhade,
mentr'el quiser, amigas, das mias dõas,
ca já m'end'el muitas deu e mui bõas,
des i terrei-lhi sempre lealdade,
mais el demanda-m'outra torpidade.

27 Joam Garcia de Guilhade

Song about an Insistent Sweetheart

Did you notice, sisters, when
my sweetheart came to talk with me,
how he insisted endlessly
until I offered him my belt?
Now he's demanding something else.

Did you notice (had it not happened!)
how, sisters, he kept insisting
until I removed my shirt's string
and gave it to him? Now he's demanding
something I really wish he hadn't.

Joam de Guilhade will always obtain
presents from me, if that is his pleasure,
for he gives me good things as well,
and my loyalty will never wane,
but now he's demanding something insane.

cantiga d'amigo

Amigas, que Deus vos valha!
quando veer meu amigo,
falade sempr' ũas outras,
enquant' el falar comigo,
    ca muitas cousas diremos,
    que ante vós non diremos.

Sei eu que por falar migo
chegará el mui coitado
e vós ide-vos chegando
lá todas per'ess'estrado,
    ca muitas cousas diremos,
    que ante vós non diremos.

28 Joam Garcia de Guilhade

Song about a Friend with Things to Say

When my friend comes,
girlfriends, please!,
talk to each other
while he talks to me,
for we say things to one another
we never would in front of others.

There will be much
he longs to say,
so when he comes,
be on your way,
for we say things to one another
we never would in front of others.

29 Joam Garcia de Guilhade

cantiga d'amigo

Cada que ven o meu amig' aqui
diz-m', aí amigas, que perd[e] o sen
por mi e diz que morre por meu ben,
mais eu ben cuido que non est assi,
ca nunca lh'eu vejo morte prender,
nen o ar vejo nunca ensandecer.

El chora muito e filha-s'a jurar
que é sandeu e quer-me fazer fis,
que por mi morr'e, pois morrer non quis,
mui ben sei eu que á ele vagar,
ca nunca lh'eu vejo morte prender,
nen o ar vejo nunca ensandecer.

Ora vejamos o que nos dirá,
pois veer viv'e pois sandeu non for;
ar direi-lh'eu: «Non morrestes d'amor?»
mais ben se quite de meu preito já,
ca nunca lh'eu vejo morte prender,
nen o ar vejo nunca ensandecer.

E ja mais nunca mi fará creer
que por mi morre, ergo se morrer.

29 Joam Garcia de Guilhade

Song for a Lover Who Would Die

Whenever my lover comes to visit,
he claims to be losing his mind
over me, and he says he's dying
with desire, but I'm unconvinced,
  for I have yet to see him dead
  or see him really lose his head.

He goes on weeping about how much
he's out of his head with love,
and for me (he says) he'd leave
this life, but I guess he's in no rush,
  for I have yet to see him dead
  or see him really lose his head.

I wonder how he will respond
when next he comes, in perfect health,
and I ask, 'Hasn't love killed you yet?';
I hope he'll give up coming around,
  for I doubt I'll ever see him dead
  or see him really lose his head.

Until he dies, not in word but in fact,
he'll only convince me he knows how to act.

30 Joam Garcia de Guilhade

cantiga d'amigo

Morr' o meu amigo d'amor
e eu non no lhi creo ben,
e el mi diz logo por en
ca verrá morrer u eu fôr,
e a mi praz de coraçon,
por veer se morre, se non.

Enviou-m'el assi dizer:
que el por mesura de mi
que o leixasse morrer aqui
e o veja, quando morrer,
e a mi praz de coraçon,
por veer se morre, se non.

Mais nunca já crea molher
que por ela morren assi,
ca nunca eu esse tal vi,
e el moira, se lhi prouguer,
e a mi praz de coraçon,
por veer se morre, se non.

30 Joam Garcia de Guilhade

Song for a Dying Admirer

My friend is dying of love
for me, but I don't believe it,
and so he says he'll come
and die right at my feet,
  and I would really like to see
  whether or not he dies for me.

He sent a message bidding
me, whom he admires,
to let him pay a visit
so I could watch him die,
  and I would really like to see
  whether or not he dies for me.

Women, don't ever believe
the suitor who would die,
for I have yet to see it,
although I wish he'd try!
  Yes, I would really like to see
  whether or not he dies for me.

31 Joam Garcia de Guilhade

cantiga d'amor

Quantos an gran coita d'amor
eno mundo, qual og' eu ei,
querrian morrer, eu o sei,
e averian én sabor.
Mais mentr' eu vos vir', mia senhor,
sempre m'eu querria viver,
e atender e atender!

Pero ja non posso guarir,
ca ja cegan os olhos meus
por vos, o non me val i Deus
nen vos; mais por vos non mentir,
enquant' eu vos, mia senhor, vir',
sempre m'eu querria viver,
e atender e atender!

E tenho que fazen mal-sen
quantos d'amor coitados son
de querer sa morte, se non
ouveron nunca d'amor ben,
com' eu faç'. E, senhor, por én
sempre m'eu quer[*r*]ia viver,
e atender e atender!

31 Joam Garcia de Guilhade

Song of a Lover Who'd Rather Not Die

Men from all around the world
who, like me, have felt love's grief,
say they would die willingly,
and I think they really would.
But, my lady, while I may see you,
  I will always want to live
  and wait and see!

And anyway there is no cure,
because I see you with blind eyes,
and God does nothing to unbind me,
nor do you, and so I'm sure
as long as I may see you, lady,
  I will always want to live
  and wait and see!

In my opinion, all of those
who have this grief and wish to die
because, as happens to me, their lives
are spent on one who doesn't love
see it all wrong. Believe me, lady,
  I will always want to live
  and wait and see!

32 Joam Garcia de Guilhade

cantiga d'amigo

Per boa fé, meu amigo,
mui ben sei eu que m'ouvestes
grand'amor e estevestes
mui gram sazon bem comigo,
mais vede-lo que vos digo:
já çafou.

Os grandes nossos amores,
que mi e vós sempr'ouvemos,
nunca lhi cima fezemos,
coma Brancafrol e Flores,
mais tempo de jogadores
já çafou.

Já eu falei en folia
con vosqu'[e] en gran cordura
e en sen e en loucura
quanto durava o dia,
mais est',ai don Jam Garçia,
já çafou.

E d'essa folia toda
já çafou!
já çafo[u] de pan de voda,
já çafou.

32 Joam Garcia de Guilhade

Song for a Distraught Lover

Believe me, friend, I know
how much you loved me and
how much I made you happy
in those days, but now
you must accept what's happened:
   it's over.

I know that you deplore
the fact we never acted
on our ardent passions
like Blanchefleur and Floris,
but the game of love we had
   is over.

I told you many things,
both in and out of my senses,
in calm and in craziness,
but now, Joam Garcia,
forget what I said and accept
   it's over.

The crazy time we lived
   is over.
The cake that was our love
   is over.

33 Joam Garcia de Guilhade

cantiga d'escarnho

Ai, dona fea, fostes-vos queixar
que vos nunca louv[o] en meu cantar;
mais ora quero fazer un cantar
 en que vos loarei toda via;
e vedes como vos quero loar:
 dona fea, velha e sandia!

Dona fea, se Deus mi pardon,
pois avedes [a]tan gran coraçon
que vos eu loe, en esta razon
 vos quero já loar toda via;
e vedes qual será a loaçon:
 dona fea, velha e sandia!

Dona fea, nunca vos eu loei
en meu trobar, pero muito trobei;
mais ora já un bon cantar farei,
 en que vos loarei toda via;
e direi-vos como vos loarei:
 dona fea, velha e sandia!

33 Joam Garcia de Guilhade

Song for an Ugly Lady

Ugly lady, you've complained
that I never sing your praise,
so I've composed a new refrain
    telling all your charms that slay me,
and this is what my heart exclaims:
    you're a crazy, old and ugly lady!

Ugly lady, your desire
is that I praise you in my rhymes,
so (God forgive me!) that is why
    I'll tell all your charms that slay me,
and this is what my heart will cry:
    you're a crazy, old and ugly lady!

Ugly lady, though I've sung
of all my loves, I never sang
a song for you, so now I'll sing
    telling of all your charms that slay me,
and this is what my heart will say:
    you're a crazy, old and ugly lady!

34 Joam Garcia de Guilhade

cantiga d'escarnho

Nunca [a]tan gran torto vi
com' eu prendo dun infançon;
e quantos ena terra son,
todo-lo te͠e por assi:
o infançon, cada que quer,
vai-se deitar con sa molher
e nulha ren non dá por mi!

E já me nunca temerá,
ca sempre me tev' en desden;
des i ar quer sa molher ben
e já sempr' i filhos fará;
si quer três filhos que fiz i,
filha-os todos pera si:
o Demo lev' o que m' en dá!

En tan gran coita viv' oj' eu,
que non poderia maior:
vai-se deitar con mia senhor,
e diz do leito que é seu
e deita-s' a dormir en paz;
des i, se filh' ou filha faz,
nono quer outorgar por meu!

34 Joam Garcia de Guilhade

Song of a Wronged Troubadour

Never have I seen such wrong
as what this nobleman does to me,
and everybody in these parts
knows exactly what I mean:
the nobleman, whenever he likes,
goes to bed with his lovely wife
and doesn't pay me the slightest heed!

He doesn't fear me in the least
but holds me in disdain instead,
for his wife, whom he adores,
will give him sons until she's dead:
what nerve he has to give his name
to the three children that I made
without giving me a shred of credit!

I feel such pain I'm sure it must
be worse than any other kind:
he takes my lady off to bed,
says she's his and spends the night
in peace without a second thought,
and when she bears a son or daughter,
he doesn't recognize it's mine!

35 Joam Garcia de Guilhade

cantiga d'escarnho

Martin jograr, que gran cousa:
já sempre con vosco pousa
    vossa molher!

Ve[e]des m' andar morrendo
e vós jazedes fodendo
    vossa molher!

Do meu mal non vos doedes,
e moir' eu, e vós fodedes
    vossa molher!

35 Joam Garcia de Guilhade

Song of a Jealous Troubadour

Martin the jongleur, what a pity
it's you who always sleeps with
 your wife!

I'm dying, as you see, of love,
while you lie down to fuck
 your wife!

My suffering matters not to you.
While I die you screw
 your wife!

cantiga d'amigo

Fui eu, madre, lavar meus cabelos
a la fonte e paguei-m'eu d'elos
e de mi, louçãa.

Fui eu, madre, lavar mias garcetas
a la fonte e paguei-m'eu d'elas
e de mi, louçãa.

A la fonte [e] paguei-m'eu d'eles,
aló achei, madr', o senhor d'eles
e de mi, louçãa.

Ante que m[e] eu d'ali partisse,
fui pagada do que m[e] el disse
e de mi, louçãa.

36 Joam Soarez Coelho

Song of the Beautiful Hair

Mother, when I was down at the spring
washing my hair I found it pretty
        and my own self fair.

Mother, when I was down at the pool
washing my hair I found it beautiful
        and my own self fair.

Washing my hair I found it beautiful
and found the man to whom it belongs
        and my own self fair.

Before I took my leave from him
I found the words he told me lovely
        and my own self fair.

37 Fernan Garcia Esgaravunha

cantiga d'escarnho

Esta ama, cuj' é Joan Coelho,
per bõas manhas que soub' aprender,
cada u for, achará bon conselho:
ca sabe ben fiar e ben tecer
e talha mui ben bragas e camisa;
e nunca vistes molher de sa guisa
que mais límpia vida sábia fazer;

Ant', é oje das molheres preçadas
que nós sabemos en nosso logar,
ca lava ben e faz bõas queijadas
e sabe ben moer e amassar
e sabe muito de bõa leiteira.
Esto non digu' eu por ben que lhi queira,
mais por que est' assi, a meu cuidar.

E seu marido, de crastar verrões,
non lh' achan par, de Burgos a Carrion,
nen [a] ela de capar galiões
fremosament', assi Deus mi pardon.
Tod' esto faz; e cata ben argueiro
e escanta ben per olh' e per calheiro
e sabe muito bõa escantaçon.

Non acharedes, en toda Castela,
graças a Deus, de que mi agora praz,
melhor ventrulho nen melhor morcela
do que a ama con sa mão faz;
e al faz ben, como diz seu marido;
faz bon souriç' e lava ben transsido
e deita ben galinha choca assaz.

37 Fernan Garcia Esgaravunha

Song in Praise of a Nursemaid Lady

The nursemaid lady of Joam Coelho
knows so many practical things
that she'd be welcome wherever she goes:
she's just great at sewing and weaving,
producing the loveliest shirts and pants,
and you've never seen a girl of her class
lead a life more wholesome and clean.

Around these parts I must confess
she's one of the finest women I know,
for she washes well, bakes good cakes,
grinds up flour and kneads smooth dough,
and no one milks cows the way she can;
I don't say this to be a gentleman
but because I really think it's so.

As for her husband, he's the best castrator
of pigs around, from Burgos to Carrion,
and nobody else could ever emasculate
roosters with her expertise and care.
And that's not all: she can read signs,
can skilfully cast an evil eye,
and knows everything about magic cures.

You will not find in all of Castile
(thank God, as this makes my tummy happy!)
sausage or blood pudding that compares
to what you'll get from this maid's hand.
There's yet more, as her husband has said:
she prepares good tripe, washes the dead,
and knows how to get any egg to hatch.

38 Juião Bolseiro

cantiga d'amigo

Fez hunha cantiga d'amor
ora meu amigo por mi,
que nunca melhor feyta vi.
Mays como x'é muy trobador,
fez hunhas lírias no son
que mi sacam o coraçon.

Muyto ben se soube buscar
por mi aly quando a fez,
en loar mi muyt'e meu prez.
Mays, de pran por xe mi matar
fez hũas lírias no son
que mi sacam o coraçon.

Per bõa fé ben baratou
de a por mi bõa fazer,
e muyto lho sey gradecer.
Mays vedes de que mi matou:
fez hũas lírias no son
que mi sacam o coraçon.

38 Juião Bolseiro

Song about a Song of Love

I've never heard a lovelier
song than the one my beloved
made for me and, being
the fine troubadour he is,
 he made a musical part
 that slew my heart.

My beloved knew, when he made
the song, how to praise me
and all of my best qualities,
and then he went and killed me
 with a musical part
 that slew my heart.

He sang the perfect words
to make me look most worthy,
which I of course enjoyed,
but now I'm quite destroyed
 thanks to a musical part
 that slew my heart.

39 Juião Bolseiro

cantiga d'amigo

Sen meu amigo manh'eu senlheyra
e sol non dormen estes olhos meus;
e quant'eu posso, peç'a luz a Deus,
e non mh-a dá per nulha maneyra.
Mays, se masesse con meu amigo,
a luz agora seria migo.

Quand'eu con meu amigo dormia,
a noyte non durava nulha ren;
e ora dur'a noyt'e vay e ven,
non ven [a] luz, nen pareç'o dia.
Mays, se masesse con meu amigo,
a luz agora seria migo.

E segundo com'a mi parece
comigo man meu lum'e meu senhor,
ven log'a luz de que non ey sabor,
e ora vay [a] noit' e ven e crece.
Mays, se masesse con meu amigo,
a luz agora seria migo.

Pater nostrus rez'eu mays de cento,
por Aquel que morreu na vera cruz,
que El mi mostre muy ced'a luz,
mays mostra-mi as noites d'Avento.
Mays, se masesse con meu amigo,
a luz agora seria migo.

39 Juião Bolseiro

Song on an Unending Night

I get so lonely without my lover
not even my eyes are able to rest:
I pray for light with every breath,
but God refuses me this favour.
  If with my lover I'd spent the night,
  it would already be light.

When I and my lover slept together,
before I knew it the night was gone,
but now the night goes on and on:
the light of the new day takes forever.
  If with my lover I'd spent the night,
  it would already be light.

According to what I have observed,
whenever my lord and love sleeps with me
then light breaks almost immediately,
ending – alas! – the short night's fervour!
  If with my lover I'd spent the night,
  it would already be light.

Sometimes I say a hundred *Our Fathers*
for the One who died on the true cross,
in hopes the new day will soon dawn,
but Advent nights are all He offers.
  If with my lover I'd spent the night,
  it would already be light.

40 Juião Bolseiro

cantiga d'amigo

Aquestas noytes tan longas,
que Deus fez en grave dia,
por min, porque as non dormho,
e porquê as non fazia
no tempo que meu amigo
soýa faltar comigo?

Porque as fez Deus tan grandes,
non posso eu dormir, coitada;
e de como son sobejas,
quisera eu outra vegada
no tenpo que meu amigo
soía falar comigo.

Porque as Deus fez tan grandes,
sen mesura desiguaaes,
e as eu dormir non posso,
porquê as non fez ataaes
no tenpo que meu amigo
soía falar comigo?

40 Juião Bolseiro

Song of the Long Nights God Made

These long nights God made
for me on a dreadful day!
Why can't I sleep and why
didn't He make them back then
  when my beloved after dark
  used to come by and talk?

Why did God make them so long
and I so sleepless and bored?
If only the nights had been
so endlessly long before
  when my beloved after dark
  used to come by and talk!

Why did God make them so long
(longer than time can measure)
in the day that I lost my sleep?
Why did He not so make them
  when my beloved after dark
  used to come by and talk?

41 Gil Perez Conde

cantiga d'escarnho

Já eu non ei por quen trobar
e já non ei en coraçon,
por que non sei já quen amar;
poren mi mingua razon,
ca mi filhou Deus mia senhor,
a que filh' o Demo maior
quantas cousas que suas son,

Como lh' outra vez já filhou
a cadeira u siia
o Filh'; e por que mi filhou
bõa senhor que avia?
E diz el que non á molher;
se a non á, pera que quer
pois tant' a bõa Maria?

Deus nunca mi a mi nada deu
e tolhe-me bõa senhor:
por esto, non creo en el eu
nen me tenh' eu por pecador,
ca me fez mia senhor perder.
Catad' o que mi foi fazer,
confiand' eu no seu amor!

Nunca se Deus mig' averrá,
se mi non der mia senhora;
mais como mi o corregerá?
Destroia-m', ante ca morra.
Om' é: tod' aqueste mal faz,
[como fez já, o gran malvaz],
e[n] Sodoma e Gomorra.

41 Gil Perez Conde

Song against God for Taking My Lady

I have no reason and no more longing
to keep on writing troubadour songs,
for now I don't know whom to love.
My inspiration was all lost
the day God took away my lady,
and so I pray the Devil will take
everything that belongs to God,

as he took, in a former age,
the chair on which the Son sat.
By what right did our God take
the loveliest lady I ever had?
He says He doesn't have a woman,
but if that's so, then for whom
was his goodly Mary fashioned?

God never gave me anything;
He only carried off my lady.
That is why I don't accept Him
nor my sins – am I to blame
that He removed my lady from me?
Take a look at how God treated
one who trusted in His grace!

I will never take God back
until He gives me back my lady,
but what He'll do, instead of that,
is make me die a wretched death.
He's a man: the hate and horror
He rained on Sodom and Gomorrah
He rains on me again today.

42 Gil Perez Conde

cantiga d'escarnho

Pôs conta el-Rei en todas fronteiras
que nen en vilas nen en carreiras
que non cômian galinhas na guerra;
ca diz que dizen as veedeiras
        que será perdimento da terra.

A concelhos e a cavaleiros
mandan comer vacas e carneiros,
mais non cômian galinhas na guerra;
ca diz que dizen os agùireiros
        que será perdimento da terra.

Cômian porcos frescos e toucinhos,
cabritos, cachaç' e ansarinhos,
mais non cômian galinhas na guerra;
ca diz que lhi dizen os devinhos
        que será perdimento da terra.

42 Gil Perez Conde

Song about What Not to Eat in War

The king sent orders to all the borders
– both in the towns and along the way –
that those in war not eat chicken meat,
because he says the diviners say
that this would mean a sure defeat.

He's told the townships and his knights
to eat all the lamb and beef they want
but not, during war, any chicken meat,
because he says the soothsayers warn
that this would mean a sure defeat.

Let them eat roast pig and bacon,
goats and ducks and pork-brain sausage
but not, while in war, any chicken meat,
because he says the seers caution
that this would mean a sure defeat.

43 Gil Perez Conde

cantiga d'escarnho

Os vossos meus maravedis, senhor,
que eu non ôuvi, que servi melhor
ou tan ben come outr' a que os dan,
ei-os d' aver enquant' eu vivo for,
ou à mia mort', ou quando mi os daran?

A vossa mia soldada, senhor Rei,
que eu servi e serv' e servirei,
com' outro quen quer a que a dan ben,
ei-a d' aver enquant' a viver ei,
ou à mia mort', ou que mi faran en?

Os vossos meus dinheiros, senhor, non
pud' eu aver, pero servidos son.
Come outros, que os an de servir,
ei-os d' aver mentr' eu viver, ou pon-
-mi-os à mia mort' o a que os vou pedir?

Ca passou temp' e trastempados son,
ouve an' e dia e quero-m' en partir.

43 Gil Perez Conde

Song of an Unpaid Soldier

Thy my money, good sir,
which I haven't received, though I served
like the others who've already been paid –
will I get it while on this earth
and alive, or only after I'm dead?

Thy my wages, good king,
whom I served and serve and will serve,
like any man promptly paid for his work –
will I get them while I'm living,
or only after I've left this world?

Thy my salary, good lord,
for service I duly performed,
at least as well as others did theirs –
will you pay it to me before
I die, or directly to my heirs?

For it's long overdue,
it's been a year and a day,
and I'd like to be on my way.

cantiga d'escarnho

Don Foão, que eu sei que á preço de livão,
vedes que fez ena guerra – daquesto soo certão:
sol que viu os genetes, come boi que fer tavão,
    sacudiu-se [e] revolveu-se, al-
    çou rab'e e foi sa via a Portugal.

Don Foão, que eu sei que á preço de ligeiro,
vedes que fez ena guerra – daquesto son verdadeiro:
sol que viu os genetes, come bezerro tenreiro,
    sacudiu-se [e] revolveu-se, al-
    çou rab'e e foi sa via a Portugal.

Don Foão, que eu sei que á prez de liveldade,
vedes que fez [e]na guerra – sabede-o por verdade:
sol que viu os genetes, come can que sal de grade,
    sacudiu-se [e] revolveu-se, al-
    çou rab'e e foi sa via a Portugal.

Song about a Noble Who Fought in Spain

Sir You-Know-Who is known to blubber.
All I know is what he did in battle:
seeing the cavalry, like a bull that's stung
    he shook his fur, turned in his tracks,
    lifted his tail and hied straight back
    to Portugal.

Sir You-Know-Who is known to cower.
All I know is what he did in combat:
seeing the cavalry, like a timid calf
    he shook his fur, turned in his tracks,
    lifted his tail and hied straight back
    to Portugal.

Sir You-Know-Who is known to fret.
All I know is what he did on the field:
seeing the cavalry, like a dog just freed
    he shook his fur, turned in his tracks,
    lifted his tail and hied straight back
    to Portugal.

sirventês (?)

Non me posso pagar tanto
do canto
das aves nen de seu son,
nen d' amor nen de mixon
nen d' armas – ca ei espanto,
por quanto
mui perigo[o]sas son,
– come dun bon galeon,
que mi alongue muit' aginha
deste demo da campinha,
u os alacrães son;
ca dentro no coraçon
senti deles a espinha!

E juro par Deus lo santo
que manto
non tragerei nen granhon,
nen terrei d' amor razon
nen d' armas, por que quebranto
e chanto
ven delas toda sazon;
mais tragerei un dormon,
e irei pela marinha
vendend' azeit' e farinha;
e fugirei do poçon
do alacran, ca eu non
lhi sei outra meezinha.

45 Alfonso X, King of Castile and León

Song of Discomfort

I'll never again be cheered
by the chirping
and delicate songs of birds
nor by love or great riches
nor by weapons (whose perils,
I confess,
have come to make me tremble),
but only by a seaworthy vessel
to carry me with all good speed
away from this land's demon
heart, full of scorpions,
as my heart knows, being sore
from all their stinging poison.

I solemnly swear by God
I'll go
without a beard or a cloak,
I'll keep my heart closed
to love, and take no weapons
(which always
result in grief and disaster):
a boat is all I ask for.
And with it I will sail
along the coast, selling
oil and flour, fleeing
until my heart is free
from every venomous sting.

Nen de lançar a tavolado
pagado
non sõo, se Deus m' ampar,
aqui, nen de bafordar;
e andar de noute armado,
sen grado
o faço, e a roldar;
ca mais me pago do mar
que de seer cavaleiro;
ca eu foi já marinheiro
e quero-m' ôi-mais guardar
do alacran, e tornar
ao que me foi primeiro.

E direi-vos un recado:
pecado
nunca me pod' enganar
que me faça já falar
en armas, ca non m' é dado
(doado
m' é de as eu razõar,
pois-las non ei a provar);
ante quer' andar sinlheiro
e ir come mercadeiro
algũa terra buscar,
u me non possan culpar
alacran negro nem veiro.

The gaming tables used to
amuse me
and I always loved to joust,
but those things bore me now,
and spending nights as an armed
guard
has also lost its appeal:
I would rather be a seaman
than keep on as a knight.
When I was young I plied
the waters, and it's my dream
to sail once more on the deep,
out of the scorpions' reach.

I still have this to tell:
the devil
will never be able to fool me
with vain thoughts of using
the weapons I've laid to rest
(best
not even to mention them,
as I won't use them again).
Alone, as a merchantman,
I'll sail in search of a land
where I know I can't be stung
by black and vicious scorpions
or by brightly coloured ones.

Cantiga de Santa Maria

ESTA É DE LOOR DE SANTA MARIA, COM' É FREMOSA E BÕA E Á GRAN PODER.

Rosas das rosas e Fror das frores,
Dona das donas, Sennor das sennores.

Rosa de beldad' e de parecer
e Fror d'alegria e de prazer,
Dona en mui piadosa seer,
Sennor en toller coitas e doores.
Rosa das rosas e Fror das frores...

Atal Sennor dev' ome muit' amar,
que de todo mal o pode guardar;
e pode-ll' os peccados perdõar,
que faz no mundo per maos sabores.
Rosa das rosas e Fror das frores...

Devemo-la muit' amar e servir,
ca punna de nos guardar de falir;
des i dos erros nos faz repentir,
que nos fazemos come pecadores.
Rosa das rosas e Fror das frores...

Esta dona que tenno por Sennor
e de que quero seer trobador,
se eu per ren poss' aver seu amor,
dou ao demo os outros amores.
Rosa das rosas e Fror das frores...

Song in Praise of Holy Mary

[This is in praise of Holy Mary, telling how she is lovely and good and does great things.]

Woman among women, Lady of ladies,
Rose among roses, Flower of flowers.

Rose of beauty and gracefulness,
Flower fresh and full of bliss,
Woman whose favour is ever with us,
Lady who takes away all sorrows.
Woman among women, Lady of ladies,
Rose among roses, Flower of flowers.

Every man should greatly love
the Lady who keeps us safe from evil
and, when we're weak, shows indulgence,
forgiving whatever sins be ours.
Woman among women, Lady of ladies,
Rose among roses, Flower of flowers.

We should greatly love and serve her,
for she struggles to preserve us,
and if we sin, she's able to turn us
from the error of our dark hours.
Woman among women, Lady of ladies,
Rose among roses, Flower of flowers.

If this Virgin I take for my Lady
and for whom, as a troubadour, I labour,
would give me her love, I would deliver
my other loves to the evil powers.
Woman among women, Lady of ladies,
Rose among roses, Flower of flowers.

47 Alfonso X, King of Castile and León

Cantiga de Santa Maria

ESTA É DE LOOR DE SANTA MARIA, DO DEPARTIMENTO QUE Á ENTRE AVE E EVA.

Entre Av' e Eva
gran departiment' á.

Ca Eva nos tolleu
o Parays' e Deus,
Ave nos y meteu;
porend', amigos meus:
Entre Av' e Eva...

Eva nos foi deitar
do dem' en sa prijon,
e Ave en sacar;
e por esta razon:
Entre Av' e Eva...

Eva nos fez perder
amor de Deus e ben,
e pois Ave aver
no-lo fez; e poren:
Entre Av' e Eva...

Eva nos ensserrou
os çeos sen chave,
e Maria britou
as portas per Ave.
Entre Av' e Eva...

47 Alfonso X, King of Castile and León

Song in Praise of Holy Mary

[This is in praise of Holy Mary, telling the difference between Ave and Eve.]

Between Ave and Eve
don't be deceived!

Through Eve we forfeited
God and his Heaven,
but Ave restored them,
and so, my friends,
between Ave and Eve
don't be deceived!

It was Eve who threw us
into Satan's prison
but Ave withdrew us,
and for this reason,
between Ave and Eve
don't be deceived!

Eve made us give up
God's grace and love,
Ave made us win
them back, and thus:
between Ave and Eve
don't be deceived!

It was Eve who closed
to us the heavens
and Mary who opened
the doors through Ave.
Between Ave and Eve
don't be deceived!

Cantiga de Santa Maria

COMO SANTA MARIA FEZE ESTAR O MONGE TREZENTOS ANOS AO CANTO DA PASSARỸA, PORQUE LLE PEDIA QUE LLE MOSTRASSE QUAL ERA O BEN QUE AVIAN OS QUE ERAN EN PARAISO.

Quena Virgen ben servirá
a Parayso irá.

E daquest' un gran miragre | vos quer' eu ora contar,
que fezo Santa Maria | por un monge, que rogar
ll'ia sempre que lle mostrasse | qual ben en Parais' á
Quena Virgen ben servirá…

E que o viss' en ssa vida | ante que fosse morrer.
E porend' a Groriosa | vedes que lle foi fazer:
fez-lo entrar en hũa orta | en que muitas vezes ja
Quena Virgen ben servirá…

Entrara; mais aquel dia | fez que hũa font' achou
mui crara e mui fremosa, | e cab' ela s'assentou.
E pois lavou mui ben sas mãos, | diss': 'Ai, Virgen, que será
Quena Virgen ben servirá…

Se verei do Parayso, | o que ch' eu muito pidi,
algun pouco de seu viço | ante que saya daqui,
e que sábia do que ben obra | que galardon averá?'
Quena Virgen ben servirá…

Tan toste que acababa | ouv' o mong' a oraçon,
oyu hũa passarinna | cantar log' en tan bon son,
que sse escaeceu seendo | e catando sempr' alá.
Quena Virgen ben servirá…

Atan gran sabor avia | daquel cant' e daquel lais,
que grandes trezentos anos | estevo assi, ou mays,
cuidando que non estevera | senon pouco, com' está
Quena Virgen ben servirá…

100

48 Alfonso X, King of Castile and León

Song of a Miracle by Holy Mary

[How Holy Mary made a monk sit still for three hundred years before a bird's singing, because he asked to be shown the wonders enjoyed by those in heaven.]

Who serves the Virgin well
will in heaven dwell.

And on this refrain I wish to tell a miraculous deed
performed by Holy Mary on behalf of a monk who pleaded
to be shown by her what kind of wonders heaven held,
Who serves the Virgin well...

and to be shown them in this life, before he died.
And so you will see what our Glorious Lady therefore did:
she made him enter a garden where he often went,
Who serves the Virgin well...

but on that day she made him find a beautiful fountain
with clear water, next to which the monk sat down.
And after washing his hands he said, 'Virgin, tell me,
Who serves the Virgin well...

may I now see heaven, and something of its pleasures
(as I've so often asked) before I leave this place?
And may I see the prize of those that follow the Way?'
Who serves the Virgin well...

Just as soon as the monk had finished saying his prayer,
he heard a bird singing such a beautiful air
he forgot himself, staring forward as if in a spell.
Who serves the Virgin well...

So very pleasant was the singing in his ears
that he stayed there for three hundred or more years,
thinking he hadn't stayed but a short while, as when
Who serves the Virgin well...

Mong' algũa vez no ano, | quando sal ao vergeu.
Des i foi-ss' a passarynna, | de que foi a el mui greu,
e diz: 'Eu daqui ir-me quero, | ca oy mais comer querrá
Quena Virgen ben servirá...

O convent'.' E foi-sse logo | e achou un gran portal
que nunca vira, e disse: | 'Ai, Santa Maria, val!
Non é est' o meu mõesteiro, | pois de mi que se fará?'
Quena Virgen ben servirá...

Des i entrou na eigreja, | e ouveron gran pavor
os monges quando o viron, | e demandou-ll' o prior,
dizend': 'Amigo, vos quen sodes | ou que buscades acá?'
Quena Virgen ben servirá...

Diss' el: 'Busco meu abade, | que agor' aqui leixey,
e o prior e os frades, | de que mi agora quitey
quando fui a aquela orta; | u seen quen mio dirá?'
Quena Virgen ben servirá...

Quand' est' oyu o abade, | teve-o por de mal sen,
e outrossi o convento; | mais des que souberon ben
de como fora esta feyto, | disseron: 'Quen oyrá
Quena Virgen ben servirá...

Nunca tan gran maravilla | como Deus por este fez
polo rogo de ssa Madre, | Virgen santa de gran prez!
E por aquesto a loemos; | mais quena non loará
Quena Virgen ben servirá...

Mais d'outra cousa que seja? | Ca, par Deus, gran dereit' é,
pois quanto nos lle pedimos | nos dá seu Fill', a la ffe,
por ela, e aqui nos mostra | o que nos depois dará'.
Quena Virgen ben servirá...

a monk, once a year, goes to pray in the garden.
When the bird had left, the monk became downhearted
and said, 'I'd better go. The convent must be waiting
Who serves the Virgin well...

for me to eat.' And so he went and found another
portal than what he knew, and said, 'Blessed Mother,
this is not my monastery. May God help me!'
Who serves the Virgin well...

Then he entered the church, frightening all the friars
by his strange appearance, until at last the prior
asked, 'Who are you and what do you seek, my friend?'
Who serves the Virgin well...

He answered, 'I seek my abbot, who was here just now,
and the prior and friars I left behind when I went down
to the garden: can you tell me where it is they went?'
Who serves the Virgin well...

When the abbot heard this, he judged the monk insane,
and so did the entire convent, but once it was explained
exactly what had happened, then they all exclaimed:
Who serves the Virgin well...

'Never was God known to do a more marvellous work
at the request of his Mother, the Virgin so very worthy.
For this we praise her, and must we not, above all else,
Who serves the Virgin well...

offer her our praise? God knows, it's only right,
since all we ask is granted by her son, the Christ,
at her urging, and here she shows us our future wealth.'
Who serves the Virgin well...

cantiga d'escarnho

Ao daian de Cález eu achei
livros que lhe levavan d' aloguer;
e o que os tragia preguntei
por eles, e respondeu-m' el: – Senher,
con estes livros que vós veedes dous
e conos outros que el ten dos sous,
fod' el per eles quanto foder quer.

E ainda vos end' eu mais direi:
macar no leito muitas [el ouver],
por quanto eu [de] sa fazenda sei,
conos livros que ten, non á molher
a que non faça que semelhen grous
os corvos, e as anguias babous,
per força de foder, se x' el quiser.

Ca non á mais, na arte do foder,
do que [è]nos livros que el ten jaz;
e el á tal sabor de os leer,
que nunca noite nen dia al faz;
e sabe d' arte do foder tan ben,
que cõnos seus livros d' artes, que el ten,
fod' el as mouras cada que lhi praz.

E mais vos contarei de seu saber,
que cõnos livros que el ten [i] faz:
manda-os ante si todos trager,
e pois que fode per eles assaz,
se molher acha que o demo ten,
assi a fode per arte e per sen,
que saca dela o demo malvaz.

49 Alfonso X, King of Castile and León

Song about the Dean's Books

I noticed a man carrying books
he'd rented from Cádiz's dean,
and when I asked to take a look,
he said, 'Sir, with the books you see
and others the dean has just like these
he's able to fuck as much as he pleases.

'And that's not all: even having
a number of women in his bed,
from what I know of the dean of Cádiz,
his books enable him to get
them all excited until they seem
like eagles, cranes or crows in heat.

'When it comes to the art of fucking,
his books have all one needs to know,
and he does absolutely nothing
but read them day and night, and so
in the art of fucking he's very wise
and fucks every Moorish dame he desires.

'There are things that he can do
with his books like no one else:
he leaves them open while he screws,
and should some woman be possessed,
he fucks her with such skill and flair
the demon doesn't have a prayer.

E, con tod' esto, ainda faz al
conos livros que ten, per bõa fé:
se acha molher que aja [o] mal
deste fogo que de Sam Marçal é,
assi [a] vai per foder encantar
que, fodendo, lhi faz ben semelhar
que é geada ou nev' e non al.

‘With his books this clever dean
can even cure St Anthony’s fire:
if a woman has this disease,
by his fucking he can charm her
until the fire begins to seem
merely snow or frost or sleet.’

50 Martin Codax

cantiga d'amigo

Ondas do mar de Vigo,
se vistes meu amigo?
E ai Deus! Se verrá cedo?

Ondas do mar levado,
se vistes meu amado?
E ai Deus! Se verrá cedo?

Se vistes meu amigo,
o por que eu sospiro?
E ai Deus! Se verrá cedo?

Se vistes meu amado,
o por que ei gran coidado?
E ai Deus! Se verrá cedo?

Seven Songs for a Beloved in Vigo

ONE

O sea waves at Vigo,
have you seen my beloved?
    Tell me: Is he coming?

O sea waves that rage,
have you seen my friend?
    Tell me: Is he coming?

Have you seen my beloved
who makes my heart troubled?
    Tell me: Is he coming?

Have you seen my friend
who makes my heart fret?
    Tell me: Is he coming?

51 Martin Codax

cantiga d'amigo

Mandad'ei comigo
ca ven meu amigo:
E irei, madr', a Vigo!

Comigu'ei mandado
ca ven meu amado:
E irei, madr', a Vigo!

Ca ven meu amigo
e ven san'e vivo:
E irei, madr', a Vigo!

Ca ven meu amado
e ven viv'e sano:
E irei, madr', a Vigo!

Ca ven san'e vivo
e d'el rei amigo:
E irei, madr', a Vigo!

Ca ven viv'e sano
e d'el rei privado:
E irei, madr', a Vigo!

TWO

Word came today:
my friend's on his way,
    and I'm going, mother, to Vigo!

Today came the tidings:
my friend is arriving,
    and I'm going, mother, to Vigo!

My friend's on his way
and is alive and well,
    and I'm going, mother, to Vigo!

My friend is arriving
and is well and alive,
    and I'm going, mother, to Vigo!

He's alive and well
and is the king's friend,
    and I'm going, mother, to Vigo!

He's well and alive
and is the king's ally,
    and I'm going, mother, to Vigo!

52 Martin Codax

cantiga d'amigo

Mia irmana fremosa, treides comigo
a la igreja de Vigo u é o mar salido:
E miraremos las ondas!

Mia irmana fremosa, treides de grado
a la igreja de Vigo u é o mar levado:
E miraremos las ondas!

A la igreja de Vig'u é o mar levado,
e verrá i, mia madre, o meu amado:
E miraremos las ondas!

A la igreja de Vig'u é o mar salido,
e verrá i, mia madre, o meu amigo:
E miraremos las ondas!

THREE

Come along, sister, come with me now
to the church in Vigo, where the waters pound,
	and we'll look at the waves!

Come with me, sister, to spend some time
at the church in Vigo, where the sea lifts high,
	and we'll look at the waves!

To the church in Vigo, where the sea lifts high,
come with me, mother – will my friend come by? –
	and we'll look at the waves!

To the church in Vigo, where the waters pound,
come along, mother – will my friend come around? –
	and we'll look at the waves!

53 Martin Codax

cantiga d'amigo

Ai Deus, se sab'ora meu amigo
com'eu senheira estou en Vigo!
E vou namorada...

Ai Deus, se sab'ora meu amado
com'eu en Vigo senheira manho!
E vou namorada...

Com'eu senheira estou en Vigo,
e nulhas gardas non ei comigo!
E vou namorada...

Com'eu senheira en Vigo manho,
e nulhas gardas migo non trago!
E vou namorada...

E nulhas gardas non ei comigo,
ergas meus olhos que choran migo!
E vou namorada...

E nulhas gardas migo non trago,
ergas meus olhos que choran ambos!
E vou namorada...

FOUR

O God, if only my friend could know
I'm here in Vigo, all alone,
and so in love!

O God, if you could only tell him
how alone I am, in Vigo, waiting,
and so in love!

How I'm here in Vigo, all alone,
without the eye of a chaperone,
and so in love!

How alone I am, in Vigo, waiting,
and not one eye watching over me,
and so in love!

Without the eye of a chaperone
– just my own eyes sore with sorrow –
and so in love!

Not one eye watching over me
– just my own eyes weeping sorely –
and so in love!

54 Martin Codax

cantiga d'amigo

Quantas sabedes amar amigo,
treides comig'a lo mar de Vigo:
E banhar nos emos nas ondas!

Quantas sabedes amar amado,
treides comig'a lo mar levado:
E banhar nos emos nas ondas!

Treides comig'a lo mar de Vigo
e veeremo'lo meu amigo:
E banhar nos emos nas ondas!

Treides comig'a lo mar levado
e veeremo'lo meu amado:
E banhar nos emos nas ondas!

54 Martin Codax

FIVE

All girls who know the meaning of love,
come with me to the sea at Vigo,
    and we'll bathe in the waves!

All girls who know what passion means,
come with me to the risen sea,
    and we'll bathe in the waves!

Come with me to the sea at Vigo
for there my beloved is sure to visit,
    and we'll bathe in the waves!

Come with me to the risen sea,
for there my beloved is sure to be,
    and we'll bathe in the waves!

55 Martin Codax

cantiga d'amigo

Eno sagrado en Vigo,
bailava corpo velido.
    Amor ei...

En Vigo, no sagrado,
bailava corpo delgado.
    Amor ei...

Bailava corpo delgado,
que nunc'ouver'amado.
    Amor ei...

Bailava corpo velido,
que nunc'ouver'amigo.
    Amor ei...

Que nunc'ouver'amigo,
ergas no sagrad', en Vigo.
    Amor ei...

Que nunc'ouver'amado,
ergas en Vigo, no sagrado.
    Amor ei...

55 Martin Codax

SIX

In Vigo by the belfry
I danced and was beautiful –
      I've fallen in love!

By the belfry in Vigo
I danced and was lovely –
      I've fallen in love!

I danced and was lovely;
I never had a beloved –
      I've fallen in love!

I danced and was beautiful;
I never had a boyfriend –
      I've fallen in love!

I never had a boyfriend
till in Vigo by the belfry –
      I've fallen in love!

I never had a beloved
till by the belfry in Vigo –
      I've fallen in love!

56 Martin Codax

cantiga d'amigo

Ai ondas que eu vin veer,
se me saberedes dizer
    porque tarda meu amigo sen min?

Ai ondas que eu vin mirar,
se me saberedes contar
    porque tarda meu amigo sen min?

56 Martin Codax

SEVEN

O waves I've come to see,
do you know the reason
    my beloved tarries without me?

O waves I've come to watch,
can you tell me why
    my beloved tarries without me?

57 Meendinho

cantiga d'amigo

Sedia-m'eu na ermida de San Simion
e cercaron-mi as ondas, que grandes son:
eu atendend'o meu amigo,
eu atendend'o meu amigo!

Estando na ermida ant'o altar,
[e] cercaron mi as ondas grandes do mar:
eu atendend'o meu amigo,
eu atendend'o meu amigo!

E cercaron-mi as ondas, que grandes son ,
non ei [i] barqueiro, nen remador:
eu atendend'o meu amigo,
eu atendend'o meu amigo!

E cercaron-mi as ondas do alto mar,
non ei [i] barqueiro, nen sei remar:
eu atendend'o meu amigo,
eu atendend'o meu amigo!

Non ei i barqueiro, nen remador,
morrerei fremosa no mar maior:
eu atendend'o meu amigo,
eu atendend'o meu amigo!

Non ei [i] barqueiro, nen sei remar
morrerei fremosa no alto mar:
eu atendend'o meu amigo,
eu atendend'o meu amigo!

57 Meendinho

Song for an Unarriving Lover

Praying at St Simon's chapel, alone,
soon I was surrounded by the rising ocean,
    waiting for my lover,
    waiting for my lover.

Before the altar of the chapel, praying,
soon I was surrounded by the ocean's waves,
    waiting for my lover,
    waiting for my lover.

Soon I was surrounded by the rising ocean,
alone, without a boatman and too weak to row,
    waiting for my lover,
    waiting for my lover.

Soon I was surrounded by the ocean's waves,
and I without a boatman to take me away,
    waiting for my lover,
    waiting for my lover.

Alone, without a boatman and too weak to row,
beautiful I'll die in the high-waving ocean,
    waiting for my lover,
    waiting for my lover.

Alone, without a boatman to take me away,
beautiful I'll die in the ocean's waves,
    waiting for my lover,
    waiting for my lover.

58 Joam Airas de Santiago

cantiga d'amigo

Todalas cousas eu vejo partir
do mund' en como soian seer,
e vej' as gentes partir de fazer
ben que soian, ¡tal tempo vos ven!,
mais non se pod' o coraçon partir
  do meu amigo de mi querer ben.

Pero que ome part' o coraçon
das cousas que ama, per bõa fe,
e parte-s' ome da terra ond' é,
e parte-s' ome d' u gran[de] prol ten,
non se pode partilo coraçon
  do meu amigo de mi [querer ben].

Todalas cousas eu vejo mudar,
mudan-s' os tempos e muda-s' o al,
muda-s' a gente en fazer ben ou mal,
mudan-s' os ventos e tod' outra ren,
mais non se pod' o coraçon mudar
  do meu amigo de mi querer ben.

58 Joam Airas de Santiago

Song of Change

I see how everything is quitting
from being what it always was,
and I see people quitting what
they were for years – time is harsh!,
but my lover can never quit
    loving me with his whole heart.

Although a man might turn his heart
away from things he's always loved,
or turn from lands where he has lived,
or turn away from his own well-being,
one thing's sure: my lover's heart
    can't turn away from loving me.

I see how everything is changing:
seasons change throughout the world,
people change for better or worse,
the winds and all things change with time,
but my lover can never change
    what his heart feels for mine.

59 Joam Airas de Santiago

cantiga d'amigo

Diz, amiga, o que mi gran ben quer
que nunca máis mi ren demandará
sol que lh' ouça quanto dizer quiser,
e mentre viver que me servirá;
  e vedes ora com' é sabedor,
  que, pois que lh' eu tod' este ben fezer,
  logu' el querra que lhi faça melhor.

Mui ben cuid' eu que con mentira ven,
pero jura que mi non quer mentir;
mais diz que fale conmigu', e por én,
mentre viver, non mi quer al pedir;
  e vedes [ora com' é sabedor,
  que, pois que lh' eu tod' este ben fezer,
  logu' el querra que lhi faça melhor].

Gran pavor ei, non me queira enganar,
pero diz el que non quer al de mí
senon falar mig', e máis demandar
mentre viver non [mi] quer, des ali;
  e vedes [ora com' é sabedor,
  que, pois que lh' eu tod' este ben fezer,
  logu' el querra que lhi faça melhor].

E esto sera mentr' o mundo for:
quant' ome máis ouver ou acabar,
tanto d' aver máis avera sabor.

Mais id', amiga, vós, por meu amor,
conmig' ali u m' el quiser falar,
ca mal mi venha se lh' eu soa for.

59 Joam Airas de Santiago

Song about a Lover Who Wants to Talk

The man who is in love with me
says he'll never demand a thing
except to be able to talk with me
and serve me as long as he lives,
        but oh, is he ever clever!
        for if I go along with him,
        he'll make me go one better.

I think he's lying through his teeth,
though he swears it's gospel truth.
He says he wants to talk, that's it,
and that he'll make no forward moves,
        but oh, is he ever clever!
        for if I go along with him,
        he'll make me go one better.

I'm deathly afraid of being deceived,
even though he claims to desire
merely the chance to talk with me
and says he'll ask no more in life,
        but oh, is he ever clever!
        for if I go along with him,
        he'll make me go one better.

So it will be till the end of time:
however much a man receives,
that much more he will require.

I beg you, sister, to come along
to where he wants to have a talk,
for if I'm alone that won't be all.

cantiga d'amigo

Diz meu amigo tanto ben de mí,
quant' el máis pod', e de meu parecer,
e os que saben que o diz assi
teen que ei eu que lhi gradecer;
  en quant' el diz non lhi gradesqu' eu ren,
  ca mi sei eu que mi paresco ben.

Diz-mi fremosa e diz-mi senhor,
e fremosa mi dira quen me vir,
e te[e]n que mi faz mui grand' amor
e que ei [eu] muito que lhi gracir;
  en quant' el diz non lhi gradesqu' eu ren,
  [ca mi sei eu que mi paresco ben].

Diz muito ben de min en seu trobar,
con gran dereit', e al vos eu direi:
teen ben quantos me lh' oen loar
que eu muito que [lhi] gradecer ei;
  en quant' el diz non lhi gradesqu' eu ren,
  [ca mi sei eu que mi paresco ben].

Ca, se eu non parecesse mui ben,
de quant' el[e] diz non diria ren.

60 Joam Airas de Santiago

Song of One Who Knows She's Good-looking

My lover speaks very well of me,
praising my looks as much as he can,
and those who hear the words he speaks
think that I must owe him thanks.
    As for his words, I thank him for nothing;
    I know that I'm indeed good-looking.

He says I'm fair and beautiful,
as all who know me naturally say,
and thus he thinks he shows great love,
for which I should, with thanks, repay.
    As for his words, I thank him for nothing;
    I know that I'm indeed good-looking.

He praises me in the songs he sings,
and rightly so, and I'll tell you more:
those who hear him praise me think
I have a lot to thank him for.
    As for his words, I thank him for nothing;
    I know that I'm indeed good-looking.

Because if I were not good-looking,
of all he says he would say nothing.

61 Joam Airas de Santiago

cantiga d'amor

A mia senhor, que eu sei muit' amar,
punhei sempre d' o seu amor gaar
e nono ouvi, mais, a meu cuidar,
non fui eu i de sén nen sabedor,
por quanto lh' eu fui amor demandar,
  ca nunca vi molher máis sen amor.

E des que a vi sempr' a muit' amei,
e sempre lhi seu amor demandei,
e nono ouvi neno averei;
mais, se cent' anos for seu servidor,
nunca lh' eu ja amor demandarei,
  ca nunca vi molher máis sen amor.

61 Joam Airas de Santiago

Song about a Loveless Lady

I know I greatly love my lady,
and for her love I truly slaved,
but never got it, having acted
without savvy and without wisdom,
thinking she might love me back –
    I've never seen a more loveless woman.

On seeing her, I loved her madly
and sought her love but never had it
and never will. If I were to serve
her hand a hundred years, I wouldn't
ever again seek love from her –
    I've never seen a more loveless woman.

pastorela

Pelo souto de Crecente
ũa pastor vi andar
muit' alongada de gente,
alçando voz a cantar,
apertando-se na saia,
quando saía la raia
do sol, nas ribas do Sar.

E as aves que voavan,
quando saía l' alvor,
todas d' amores cantavan
pelos ramos d' arredor;
mais non sei tal qu' i 'stevesse,
que en al cuidar podesse
senon todo en amor.

Ali 'stivi eu mui quedo,
quis falar e non ousei,
empero dix' a gran medo:
– Mia senhor, falar-vos-ei
un pouco, se mi ascuitardes,
e ir-m' ei quando mandardes,
máis aqui non [e]starei.

– Senhor, por Santa Maria,
non estedes máis aqui,
mais ide-vos vossa via,
faredes mesura i;
ca os que aqui chegaren,
pois que vos aqui acharen,
ben diran que máis ouv' i.

62 Joam Airas de Santiago

Pastoral Song

In the woods outside Crecente
I saw a shepherdess walking along
ahead of where my own feet went;
she gently raised her voice in song,
holding her dress against her breast,
as the sun's rays started to break
over the banks of the Sar.

And the birds that flew around us
as the sun was slowly lifting
all began to sing of love
on the branches that hung low,
and I don't know of any soul
who in that place and at that moment
would not have thought of love.

Wanting to speak but too afraid,
for a long time I merely watched,
and finally, full of fear, I said:
'Madam, I'd like the chance to talk
if you'll be kind enough to listen,
and when you wish, I promise to leave
without insisting on staying longer.'

'Sir,' she said, 'by Holy Mary,
please don't stay another minute
but just keep going on your way,
thereby showing respect for me,
because if anyone should appear
and see you talking with me here,
they'll say they saw much more.'

63 Joam Airas de Santiago

cantiga d'escarnho

Ũa dona – non digu' eu qual –
non agùirou ogano mal:
polas oitavas de Natal
ia por sa missa oir,
e [ouv'] un corvo carnaçal
  e non quis da casa sair.

A dona mui de coraçon
oira sa missa enton,
e foi por oir o sarmon
e vedes que lho foi partir:
ouve sigo un corv' a caron
  e non quis da casa sair.

A dona disse: 'Que sera?
E i o clerigu' está ja
revesti' e maldizer-mi-á,
se me na igreja non vir'.
E diss[e] o corvo: 'qua, ca'
  e non quis da casa sair.

Nunca taes agoiros vi,
des aquel dia que naci,
com' aquest' ano ouv' aqui;
e ela quis provar de s' ir,
e ou[v'] un corvo sobre sí
  e non quis da casa sair.

63 Joam Airas de Santiago

Song about a Strange Omen

A woman whose name I'll save
interpreted well an omen
received in the Christmas octave:
on leaving for Mass she noticed
a hungry, carnivorous crow
  and decided to stay at home.

The woman, highly fervent,
wanted to hear Mass and hoped
to arrive in time for the sermon,
but look what kept her from going:
she had in her company a crow
  and decided to stay at home.

The woman cried, 'Who'll save me?
The priest has donned his robes
by now and will curse me greatly
if at church I don't show.'
'Caw, caw!' exclaimed the crow,
  and she decided to stay at home.

Never since I was christened
have I ever seen such omens
as what occurred this Christmas:
she tried to go to the Holy
Mass but was charmed by a crow
  and decided to stay at home.

64 Joam Vasquiz de Talaveira

cantiga d'escarnho

O que veer quiser, ai, cavaleiro,
Maria Pérez, leve algun dinheiro;
senon, non poderá i adubar prol.

Quena veer quiser ao serão,
Maria Pérez, lev' algu' en sa mão;
senon, non poderá i adubar prol.

Tod' ome que a ir queira veer suso,
Maria Pérez, lev' algo de juso;
senon, non poderá i adubar prol.

64 Joam Vasquiz de Talaveira

Song on How to Pay a Visit

Should any gentleman wish to call
on Maria Perez, take money along,
  or else you're not going to get very far.

Whoever would pay an evening visit
to Maria Perez, have money in fist,
  or else you're not going to get very far.

Every man who wants to converse
with Maria Perez, take a full purse,
  or else you're not going to get very far.

65 Lourenço and Joam Vasquiz

cantiga d'escarnho

Johan Vaasquez, moiro por saber
de vós porque me leixastes o trobar,
ou se foy el vos primeiro leixar.
Ca, vedes, aque ouço a todos dizer
ca o trobar acordou-s'en atal
qu'estava vosco en pecado mortal,
e leixa-vos por se non perder.

Lourenço tu vẽes por aprender
de min, e eu non ch'o quero negar:
eu trobo ben quando quero trobar,
p'ro non o quero sempre fazer.
Mais di-me tu, que trobas desigual,
se te deitam por én de Portugal,
ou mataste homen ou roubaste aver.

Johan Vaasquez, nunca roubei rem
nen matey homen nen ar mereci
por que mi deitassem, mais vin aqui
por gãar algo, e po[i]s sei iguar-mi ben
como o trobar vosso; maes estou
que se predia tan vosqu', e quitou-
-sse de vós, e non trobades por én.

65 Lourenço and Joam Vasquiz

Song of the Troubadour's Art On Finding Itself in Sin

– Joam Vasquiz, I'm dying to know
why you've let go of the troubadour's art,
or is it, as people have remarked,
that the art of troubadouring let you go?
For it seems our art at long last knew
that it was in mortal sin with you
and left you to keep from coming to woe.

– Lourenço, don't misunderstand:
I still compose troubadour songs,
but only when the urge is strong.
And tell me now, if you can,
you whose songs are the poorest of all:
is that why you had to leave Portugal,
or because you robbed or killed a man?

– Joam Vasquiz, I've done no wrong
to any man that I would deserve
to be sent out. I've come to earn
some money here as a troubadour
no worse than you; but now it seems
the troubadour's art, fleeing from sin,
has left you so that you sing no more.

cantiga d'amor

Os que non amam nen saben d'amor
fazen perder aos que amor am.
Vedes porque: quand'ant'as donas vam,
juram que morren por elas d'amor,
e elas saben poys que non é 'ssy;
e por esto perç'eu e os que ben
lealmente aman, segundo meu sén.

Ca sse elas soubessen os que an
ben verdadeyramente grand'amor,
d'alguen sse doeria ssa senhor,
mays, por aqueles que o jurad'am,
cuydan-ss'elas que todus taes son;
e por esto perç'eu e os que ben
[lealmente aman, segundo meu sén.]

E aqueles que ja medo non an
que lhis faça coita sofrer amor,
vẽen ant'elas e juran melhor
ou tan ben come os que amor an,
e elas non saben quaes creer;
e por [esto perç'eu e os que ben
lealmente aman, segundo meu sén.]

E os ben desanparadus d'amor
juran que morren con amor que an,
sseend'ant'elas, e menten de pran;
mays, quand'ar vẽen os que an amor,
ja elas cuydan que vẽen mentir;
e por esto perç'eu e os que ben
[lealmente aman, segundo meu sén.]

66 Joam Baveca

Song against Those Who Falsely Swear Love

Those whose love is false or feigned
do wrong to us who truly love,
for when they go before the ladies,
they swear they're dying of love for them,
and the ladies know it isn't so,
    and that is why – I have no doubt –
    we who truly love lose out.

If they knew the pure intention
of those of us whose love is true,
these ladies would I'm sure be moved,
but those who falsely swear affection
make them think we're all that way,
    and that is why – I have no doubt –
    we who truly love lose out.

Those who do not need to fear
that love might ever cause them anguish
can swear devotion just as well
or better than those who really feel,
and the ladies don't know who to believe,
    and that is why – I have no doubt –
    we who truly love lose out.

Those who don't know what love is
swear they love to the point of dying
before the ladies, baldly lying,
and faced by those who really love them,
the ladies think we're lying too,
    and that is why – I have no doubt –
    we who truly love lose out.

67 Joam Baveca

cantiga d'amigo

– Filha, de grado queria saber
de voss'amigu'e de vós hunha ren:
como vus vay ou como vus aven.
– Eu vo-lo quero, mha madre, dizer:
quero lh'eu ben e que-lo el a mi,
e ben vus digo que non á mays hy.

– Filha, non sey se á hi mays, se non,
mays vejo-vus sempre con el falar
e vejo vós chorar e el chorar.
– Non vus terrey, madre, hy outra razon:
quero lh'eu ben [e que-lo el a mi,
e ben vus digo que non á mays hy.]

– Se mh-o negardes, filha, pesar-mh-á,
ca, se mays á hy feyt', a como quer,
outro consselh'avemus hi mester.
– Ja vus eu dixi, madre, quant'i á:
quero-lh'eu ben [e que-lo el a mi,
e ben vus digo que non á mays hy.]

67 Joam Baveca

Song about a Suspicious Mother

– Daughter, I would like to know
something about you and your friend:
how does it go?, where will it end?
– *I'll tell you, Mother, how it goes:*
he loves me and I love him,
and I swear that's all there is.

– I wonder, daughter, if there's more,
for every time your friend comes by
I see you weep and see him cry.
– *Mother, it's like I said before:*
he loves me and I love him,
and I swear that's all there is.

– Beloved daughter, I would be sad
if there is something you conceal,
for then we would need different counsel.
– *Mother, it's as I've already said:*
he loves me and I love him,
and I swear that's all there is.

cantiga d'amigo

Pois nossas madres vam a San Simon
de Val de Prados candeas queimar,
nós, as meninhas, punhemos d'andar
con nossas madres, e elas enton
queimen candeas por nós e por si
e nós, meninhas, bailaremos i.

Nossos amigos todos lá iram
por nos veer e andaremos nós
bailand'ant'eles, fremosas, en cós,
e nossas madres, pois que alá van,
queimen candeas por nós e por si
e nós, meninhas, bailaremos i.

Nossos amigos iran por cousir
como bailamos e poden veer
bailar moças de [mui] bon parecer,
e nossas madres, pois lá queren ir,
queimen candeas por nós e por si
e nós, meninhas, bailaremos i.

Song in Favour of a Pilgrimage

Since our mothers are going to St Simon's
in Val de Prados to burn votive candles,
let's go, girls, and visit the shrine
along with our mothers, who in the chapel
  can burn some candles for us and themselves
  while we, girls, dance on the steps.

All of our boyfriends will journey there
in order to see us, so why don't we go
and dance, removing our cloaks to look fair?
And our mothers will also be there and so
  can burn some candles for us and themselves
  while we, girls, dance on the steps.

Our boyfriends will be there to observe
how well we dance, and as they look
at our fine figures before the church,
our dear mothers – who'll be there too –
  can burn some candles for us and themselves
  while we, girls, dance on the steps.

69 Roi Paez de Ribela

cantiga d'escarnho

Ven un ricome das truitas,
que compra duas por muitas,
e coz'end'a ũa.

Por quanto xi quer ebenas,
compra en duas pequenas,
e coz'end'a ũa.

Venden cen truitas vivas,
e compra en duas cativas,
e coz'end'a ũa.

E, u as venden bolindo,
vai-s'en con duas friindo,
e coz'end'a ũa.

69 Roi Paez de Ribela

Song about a Rich Man's Trout

If a rich man wants trout,
he buys two at a discount
  and cooks one of them.

Although he likes big fish,
he buys two of the littlest
  and cooks one of them.

They sell trouts of all sorts
and he buys the two worst
  and cooks one of them.

He buys what's cheap,
two fish that reek,
  and cooks one of them.

70 Roi Paez de Ribela

cantiga d'escarnho

Preguntad' un ricome
mui rico, que mal come,
    por que o faz.

El, de fam' e de sede,
mata ome, beno sabede.
    Por que o faz?

Mal com' e faz nemiga;
dizede-lhi que o diga
    por que o faz.

70 Roi Paez de Ribela

Song about What a Rich Man Eats

Ask a man who is rich
and eats what's unfit:
        what for?

Out of thirst and hunger
the rich man kills others.
        What for?

He eats and acts badly,
so go and ask him:
        what for?

71 Roi Paez de Ribela

cantiga d'escarnho

A donzela de Biscaia
ainda mi a preito saia
de noit' ou lũar!

Pois m' agora assi desdenha,
ainda mi a preito venha
de noit' ou lũar!

Pois dela são maltreito
ainda mi venha a preito
de noit' ou lũar!

71 Roi Paez de Ribela

Song about a Disdainful Damsel

May the damsel of Biscay
still make our tryst today
    under the light of the moon!

Although she now disdains me,
I'll gladly find her waiting
    under the light of the moon!

Although she treats me meanly,
she's welcome to come meet me
    under the light of the moon!

72 Roi Fernandez

cantiga d'amor

Quand' eu vejo las ondas
e las muyt' altas ribas,
logo mi veen ondas
al cor pola velyda:
maldito se[j]a l' mare,
que mi faz tanto male!

Nunca ve[j]o las ondas
nen as [muit'] altas rocas
que mi non venhan ondas
al' cor pola fremosa:
maldito se[j]a l' mare,
que mi faz tanto male!

Se eu vejo las ondas
e ve[j]o las costeyras,
logo mi veen ondas
al cor pola ben feyta:
maldito se[j]a l' mare,
que mi faz tanto male!

72 Roi Fernandez

Song against the Sea

Whenever I look at the waves
that break below the bluffs,
I feel a pounding of waves
in my heart for the one I loved.
    Damn the sea
    that makes me grieve!

I never look at the waves
that beat against the shores
without being pounded by waves
in my heart for the one I adored.
    Damn the sea
    that makes me grieve!

Each time I look at the waves
that crash into the cliffs,
I feel a pounding of waves
in my heart for the one I miss.
    Damn the sea
    that makes me grieve!

73 Roi Fernandez

cantiga d'amor

Ora começa o meu mal
de que ja non temia ren,
e cuidava que m' ia ben.
E todo se tornou en mal:
    ca o dem' agora d'amor
    me fez filhar outra senhor!

E ja dormia todo meu
sono, e ja non era fol,
e podia fazer mia prol.
Mais lo poder ja non é meu:
    ca o dem' agora d'amor
    me fez filhar outra senhor!

Que ledo me fezera ja,
quando s' Amor de min quitou
un pouco, que mi-a min leixou.
Mais d'outra guisa me vai ja:
    ca o dem' agora d'amor
    me fez filhar outra senhor!

E non se dev' om' alegrar
muito de ren que poss' aver,
ca eu, que o quige fazer,
non ei ja de que m' alegrar:
    ca o dem' agora d'amor
    me fez filhar outra senhor!

Ao dem' acomend' eu amor;
e bẽeiga Deus a senhor
de que non será sabedor
nulh' om', enquant' eu vivo for'.

73 Roi Fernandez

Song of a Man in Trouble

Time again for troubles!
It seemed things were going
well in my life, but no –
already I'm in for trouble,
    the demon of love having led me
    to take on another lady.

I'd learned once more to rule
my emotions, heart and mind
and to sleep the entire night,
but then I was overruled,
    the demon of love having led me
    to take on another lady.

All my happiness returned
the very same day that love
at long last left me alone,
but now the tables are turned,
    the demon of love having led me
    to take on another lady.

How stupid it is to say
I'm going to do this and that,
for I can have hundreds of plans
but won't have the final say
    if the demon of love has led me
    to take on another lady.

Love can go to the devil,
and may God bless each lady
who will stay away from men
for as long as I am living.

cantiga d'amor

Hũa dona, que eu quero gram ben,
por mal de mi, par Deus, que non por al,
pero que sempre mi fez e faz mal
e fará, direy-vo-lo que m' aven:
mar, nen terra, nen prazer, nen pesar,
nen ben, nen mal non mh-a podem quytar

Do coraçon, e que será de mi?
Morto son, sse çedo non morrer;
ela já nunca ben mh-á de fazer,
mays sempre mal, e, pero est' assy,
mar, nen terra, nen prazer, nen pesar,
nen ben, nen mal non mh-a podem quytar

Do coraçon; ora mi vay peyor,
ca mi ven d' ela, por vos non mentir,
mal, se a vej', e mal, sse a non vir,
que de coytas [as] mays cuyd' a mayor;
mar, nen terra, nen prazer, nen pesar,
nen ben, nen mal non mh-a podem quytar.

74 Pai Gomez Charinho

Song about an Occupied Heart

There is a woman I love helplessly
(God knows why but for my own disgrace),
who always was and is and will be
pain to me. What would you do in my place?
    For neither sea nor land, nor faith nor doubt,
    nor pleasure nor sorrow can tear her out

of my heart – and what will become of me?
I'll keep on dying, unless I die really.
Loving her never yet made me happy,
only miserable, but what can free me?
    For neither sea nor land, nor faith nor doubt,
    nor pleasure nor sorrow can tear her out

of my heart – and what torments me the most,
I'll be honest, is knowing I will suffer
whether I see her or whether I don't.
Is there any escape from the curse of a lover
    whom neither sea nor land, nor faith nor doubt,
    nor pleasure nor sorrow can tear out?

75 Pai Gomez Charinho

cantiga d'amor

Quantos oj' andan eno mar aqui
cuidan que coita no mundo non á
se non do mar, ne[*n*] an outro mal ja;
mais d'outra guisa contec(e) og(e) a mi:
coita d'amor me faz escaecer
a mui gran coita do mar, e tẽer

Pola mayor coita de quantas son,
coita d'amor, a que'-na Deus quer dar.
E é gran coita de mort' a do mar,
mais non é tal; e por esta razon
coita d'amor me faz escaecer
a mui gran coita do mar, e tẽer

Pola mayor coita, per bõa fé,
de quantas foron, nen son, nen seran.
E estes outros que amor non an,
dizen que non; mais eu direi qual é:
coita d'amor me faz escaecer
a mui gran coita do mar, e tẽer

Por mayor coita a que faz perder
coita do mar, que faz muitos morrer!

75 Pai Gomez Charinho

Song about the Pain of Love and Sea

Those who spend their lives at sea
think there is no pain in the world
as great as their pain, and no fate worse
than a seaman's fate, but consider me:
    the pain of love made me forget
    the pain of sea, so cruel and yet

As nothing next to that greatest pain,
the pain of love that God ordains.
The pain of sea is a pain unto death,
but I discovered it can't compare
    to the pain of love, which made me forget
    my seaman's pain, terrible and yet

As nothing next to the greatest of all
the pains that are, were or will come.
Those who have never been in love
can't know the pain I feel, because
    the pain of love makes one forget
    all other pains, cruel and yet

As nothing next to the pain that exceeds
even the deathly pain of sea.

cantiga d'amigo

As frores do meu amigo
briosas van no navio
E van-s[e] as frores
d'aqui ben con meus amores!
Idas son as frores
d'aqui ben con meus amores.

As frores do meu amado
briosas van [e]no barco!
E van-s[e] as frores
d'aqui ben con meus amores!
Idas son as frores
d'aqui ben con meus amores!

Briosas van no navio
pera chegar ao ferido.
E van-s[e] as frores
d'aqui ben con meus amores!
Idas son as frores
d'aqui ben con meus amores!

Briosas van eno barco
pera chegar ao fossado.
E van-s[e] as frores
d'aqui ben con meus amores!
Idas son as frores
d'aqui ben con meus amores!

Pera chegar ao ferido,
servir mi, corpo velido.
E van-s[e] as frores
d'aqui ben con meus amores!
Idas son as frores
d'aqui ben con meus amores!

76 Pai Gomez Charinho

Song of the Parting Flowers

The flowers of my lover
bravely board ship,
    and they're leaving now
    along with my love!
    Gone are the flowers
    along with my love!

The flowers of my friend
go bravely aboard,
    and they're leaving now
    along with my love!
    Gone are the flowers
    along with my love!

They bravely board ship
to sail off to battle,
    and they're leaving now
    along with my love!
    Gone are the flowers
    along with my love!

They go bravely aboard
to sail off to war,
    and they're leaving now
    along with my love!
    Gone are the flowers
    along with my love!

To sail off to battle
to serve me, his beauty,
    and they're leaving now
    along with my love!
    Gone are the flowers
    along with my love!

Pera chegar ao fossado,
servir mi, corpo loado.
E van-s[e] as frores
d'aqui ben con meus amores!
Idas son as frores
d'aqui ben con meus amores!

To sail off to war
to serve me, his lady,
    and they're leaving now
    along with my love!
    Gone are the flowers
    along with my love!

77 Pai Gomez Charinho

cantiga d'amigo

Disseron-m'oj',ai amiga, que non
é meu amig'almirante do mar
e meu coraçon já pode folgar
e dormir já, e por esta razon
o que do mar meu amigo sacou
saque-o Deus de coitas qu[e] afogou.

Mui ben é a mi, ca já non andarei
triste por vento que veja fazer,
nen por tormenta non ei de perder
o sono, amiga, mais, se foi el-rei
o que do mar meu amigo sacou
saque-o Deus de coitas qu[e] afogou.

Mui ben é a mi, ca já cada que vir
algun ome de fronteira chegar,
non ei medo que me diga pesar,
mais, porque m'el fez ben, sen lho pedir,
o que do mar meu amigo sacou
saque-o Deus de coitas qu[e] afogou.

77 Pai Gomez Charinho

Song for a Lover Who Went to Sea

Listen, sister! They told me
my lover is admiral over the sea
no longer, and now I can sleep
with a quiet heart, and so
    whoever freed my lover from the ocean,
    may God free him from all love's sorrows.

No news could be more relieving,
sister! Now I won't worry
when the wind is high, and storms
won't rob my sleep. If the king
    was who freed my lover from the ocean,
    may God free him from all love's sorrows.

How relieved I am! My thoughts
will no longer tremble each time
they announce the sailors who've died.
Because of the joy he brought me,
    whoever freed my lover from the ocean,
    may God free him from all love's sorrows.

cantiga d'amigo

Moir', amiga, desejando
meu amigu'e vós no vosso
mi falades e non posso
estar sempr' en esto falando,
mais queredes falar migo?
falemos no meu amigo.

Queredes que todavia
eno voss'amigo fale
vosqu'e, se non, que me cale,
e non poss'eu cada dia,
mais queredes falar migo?
falemos no meu amigo.

Amiga, sempre queredes
que fale vosqu'e falades
no voss'amigu'e cuidades
que poss'eu; non o cuidedes,
mais queredes falar migo?
falemos no meu amigo.

Non avedes d'al cuidado,
sol que eu vosco ben diga
do voss'amigu'e, amiga,
non poss'eu, nen é guisado,
mais queredes falar migo?
falemos no meu amigo.

Song about the Theme of Conversation

My heart is dying of desire
for my friend, as you, sister,
talk of yours, and I'm tired
of us always talking about him.
    If you want to talk with me,
    let my boyfriend be the theme.

Still you insist we keep on
talking about your friend,
unless I prefer to keep quiet,
and it's like this every day.
    If you want to talk with me,
    let my boyfriend be the theme.

Sister, you've always wanted
to talk and me to talk too
about your friend, for you thought
that I didn't mind, but I do.
    If you want to talk with me,
    let my boyfriend be the theme.

You worry about nothing besides
my words concerning your friend,
if they're good or bad, but I've
had enough, you know it's not fair.
    If you want to talk with me,
    let my boyfriend be the theme.

79 Joam Lobeira

cantiga d'amor

Senhor genta,
mi[n] tormenta
voss'amor em guisa tal
que tormenta
que su senta
outra non m'é ben, nen mal,
mays la vossa m'é mortal:
Le[o]noreta,
fin rosetta,
bella sobre toda fror,
fin roseta,
non me metta
en tal coi[ta] voss'amor!

Das que vejo
non desejo
outra senhor se vós non,
e desejo,
tan sobejo,
mataria hũ(u) leom,
senhor do meu coraçon:
Leonoreta,
fin roseta,
bella sobre toda fror,
fin roseta,
non me metta
en tal coi[ta] voss'amor!

79 Joam Lobeira

Song for Leonorette

Lovely lady,
you torment me
with your love in such a way
my mind, tormented,
can't remember
other loves from former days:
your love's fatal, I'm afraid.
Leonorette,
fine rosette,
lovelier than any flower;
fine rosette,
do no let
me fall too far into your power!

I admire
but don't desire
any hand except for yours,
which I desire
with such fire
I could stop a lion short,
lady whom my heart adores!
Leonorette,
fine rosette,
lovelier than any flower;
fine rosette,
do no let
me fall too far into your power!

Mha ventura
en loucura
me meteo de vos amar;
é loucura,
que me dura,
que me non poss(o) en quitar,
ay fremosura sem par:
Leonoreta,
fin roseta,
bella sobre toda fror,
fin roseta,
non me metta
en tal coi[ta] voss'amor!

It was chance that
acting madly
made me fall in love with you,
and the madness
keeps on lasting:
there is nothing I can do
before such beauty, pure and true!
Leonorette,
fine rosette,
lovelier than any flower;
fine rosette,
do no let
me fall too far into your power!

80 Roi Queimado

cantiga d'amor

Preguntou Johan Garcia
da morte de que morria;
e dixe-lh'eu todavia:
'A morte d'esto se mata:
Guiomar Affonso Gata
est a dona que me mata.'

Pois que m'ouve preguntado
de que era tan coitado,
dixe-lh'eu este recado:
'A morte d'esto xe mata:
Guiomar Affonso Gata
est a dona que me mata.'

Dixe-lh'eu 'ja vus digo
a coita que ei comigo
per bõa fé, meu amigo:
A morte d'esto se mata:
Guiomar Affonso Gata
est a dona que me mata.'

80 Roi Queimado

Song of the Death I'm Dying

When Joam Garcia inquired
what death it is I'm dying,
I answered in this wise:
    'I'm dying a death of passion
    for Guiomar Affonso Gata,
    woman and assassin.'

He kept wanting to know
the nature of my woe,
and this is what I told:
    'I'm dying a death of passion
    for Guiomar Affonso Gata,
    woman and assassin.'

I said to him, 'My friend,
I will indeed explain
the reason for my pain:
    I'm dying a death of passion
    for Guiomar Affonso Gata,
    woman and assassin.'

81 Roi Queimado

cantiga d'amor

Pois [*que*] eu ora morto for',
sei ben ca dirá mia senhor:
«Eu sõo Guiomar Affonso!»

Pois souber' mui ben ca morri
por ela, sei ca dirá (a)ssi:
«Eu sõo Guiomar Affonso!»

Pois que eu morrer', filhará
enton o seu queix' e dirá:
«Eu sõo Guiomar Affonso!»

81 Roi Queimado

Song for When I Die

When they tell her I have died,
this will be my love's reply:
    'Guiomar Affonso is my name!'

When she knows I've died for her,
this is what she'll say for sure:
    'Guiomar Affonso is my name!'

When I die, she's going to lay
her chin in palm and then exclaim:
    'Guiomar Affonso is my name!'

cantiga d'escarnho

Roy [Q]ueymado morreu c*on* amor
en se*us* cantares, par [S]anta Maria!
por hunha dona que gra*n* ben queria,
e por se meter por mays trobador,
por que lh' ela non quis ben fazer,
feze s' el en se*us* cantares morrer,
mays resurgiu depoys ao tercer dia.

Esto fez el p*or* hunha sa senhor
que quer gram ben, e mays v*us* en dirya:
p*or* que cuyda que faz hi maestria,
en*os* cantares que fez á sabor
de morrer hy e des y d' ar vyver.
Esto faz el que xo pode fazer,
mays outr' omen p*er* ren nono faria.

E non á ja de sa morte pavor,
se non sa morte mays la temeria,
mays sabe ben, per sa sabedoria,
que vyverá desquando morto for,
e faz en seu cantar morte p*re*nder,
des y ar vyv' e vedes que poder
que lhi D*eu*s deu! Mays queno cuydaria!

E se mi D*eu*s a min desse poder,
qual oj' el á, poys morrer, de viver,
ja mays morte nu*n*ca temeria!

82 Pero Garcia Burgalês

Song for a Troubadour Who Dies and Dies

Roi Queimado has died of love
(he swears by heaven in his verses)
because the loved one did not love him.
In his effort to convince her
what a great troubadour he is,
he died for her in a refrain,
but three days later was back again.

He's a supernatural troubadour!
Determined to convince his lady
that he truly does adore her
and can write great songs of love,
deathless dying became quite normal.
Surely no other creature on earth
can depart at will, and at will return.

Of his death he has no fear
– imagine, if he did, how great! –
because he knows he has that flair
for resurrecting from the grave.
Raising the dead is God's affair,
but Roi Queimado, with his verses,
can bring on death and then reverse it.

If I, like Roi, could always depend
on living tomorrow after dying today,
perhaps I too would not fear death.

83 Pero Garcia Burgalês

cantiga d'escarnho

Dom'na Maria [N]egra, ben talhada,
dizem que sodes de min namorada!
        Se me ben queredes,
por Deus, amiga, que m' oy sorrabedes,
        se me ben queredes.

Poys eu tanto por voss' amor ey f[eyt]o,
aly hu vos migo talhastes preyto!
        Se me ben queredes,
[por Deus, amiga, que m' oy sorrabedes,
        se me ben queredes].

Por non vĩir a min soa, sinlheyra,
venha convosc' a vossa covilheyra!
        Se me ben queredes,
[por Deus, amiga, que m' oy sorrabedes,
        se me ben queredes].

Poys m' eu por vos de peydos vaso,
aly hu vos migo talhastes prazo!
        Se me ben queredes,
[por Deus, amiga, que m' oy sorrabedes,
        se me ben queredes].

83 Pero Garcia Burgalês

Song for a Lady in Love with Me

Maria Negra, most fair lady,
I hear that you're in love with me.
  If you love me, then you're lucky,
    and I dare say
  you'll be after my ass today.

How very much I strove to earn
this tryst I surely don't deserve!
  If you love me, then you're lucky,
    and I dare say
  you'll be after my ass today.

In order not to journey alone,
why not bring your maid along?
  If you love me, then you're lucky,
    and I dare say
  you'll be after my ass today.

How much I farted when I heard
of this tryst I don't deserve!
  If you love me, then you're lucky,
    and I dare say
  you'll be after my ass today.

cantiga d'escarnho

Maria [N]egra, desventuyrada,
e por que quer tantas pissas co*m*prar,
poys lhe na mã[o] no*n* quere*n* durar,
e lh' assi morre*n* aa malfada[da]?
E nun caralho grande que co*m*prou,
oonte ao serã[o] o esfolou,
e outra pissa ten ja amormada.

E ja ela é probe tornada,
compra*n*do pissas, vedes q*ue* ventuyra!
Pis[s]a que compra pouco lhe dura,
sol que a mete na sa pou[s]ada,
ca lhi conven que ali moyra e*n*tom
de polmoeyra ou de torzilhon,
ou, per for[ç]a, fica e*n*de aaguada.

Muit' é p*er* aventuyra menguada
de tantas pis[s]as no ano perder,
que compra caras poys lha [v]a*n* morrer;
e est' é pola casa molhada
e*n* que as mete, na estrabaria.
Poys lhe morren, a velha sandia,
per pis[s]as, será e*n* terra deytada.

84 Pero Garcia Burgalês

Song about a Sad, Impoverished Lady

Maria Negra is looking sadder:
why does she buy so many cocks
when in her hand they always rot,
dying in haste and without grandeur?
A big dick purchased yesterday
was by evening completely flayed,
and another cock already has glanders.

She's gotten rather poor in the process
of buying cocks – how sad her lot!
The cocks she buys never last long
after she sticks them in her hospice,
because they always end up dying
of gripes or heaves, or else stop trying,
having worked to sheer exhaustion.

Sadly her funds have been wiped out
from all the cocks she buys in a year:
they cost her dear, then die on her,
and this is because of the damp house
she sticks them in, a smelly stable.
When they die, the crazy old lady
lies there, cockless, on the ground.

cantiga d'escarnho

Que muyto mi de [F]ernam [D]iaz praz,
que fez el Rey [D]on [A]fonso meyrinho,
e non cata parente nen vezinho,
con sabor de teela t[er]ra en paz.
Se o pode por mal feytor saber,
vay sobr' el, e se o pode colher
na mão, logo del justiça faz.

E por que á [D]on [F]ernando gra*n* prez
das gentes todas de mui justiceyro,
o fez el Rey meyrinho des Viveyro
ata [C]arron, ond' outro nu*n*ca fez;
e se ouve de mal feitor falar,
vay sobr' el, e no*n* lhi pod' escapar,
e faz lhi mal jogo p*or* hũa vez.

E cuydará del queno vir aqui,
que o vir andar assy calado,
ca non sabe p*ar*te nen mandado
de tal justiça faz*er* qual [l]h'eu vi:
leixou a gente adormecer enton
e trasnoytou sobr' u*n* hom' a Leon
e fez sobr' el gra*n* justiça logu' i.

85 Pero Garcia Burgalês

Song about a Sheriff Who Lays Down the Law

I'm glad that King Alfonso thought
to make Fernando Diaz sheriff,
for he spares neither friend nor relative
but always keeps the land quite calm:
if a wrongdoer comes to his notice,
he lays down the law, and getting hold
of the man, he really lays it on.

Because Fernando is considered
by all around to be very fair,
he was made sheriff from Viveiro
to Carrion, where no one ever served,
and if he hears a wrongdoer's near,
he lays down the law, going in search
of the man, to deal him his just deserts.

Let every visiting man take heed
to keep out of sight, avoiding misdeeds,
for with Fernando you've no idea
of the brutal justice I have seen:
he waited till all were asleep and then
spent the whole night on a man in León,
laying on a justice you wouldn't believe!

86 Pero Garcia Burgalês

cantiga d'escarnho

Don [F]ernando, pero mi mal digades,
quero v*us* eu ora desenganar,
ca ou[ç]' as gentes de vos posfa[ç]ar
de cavalgar, de que v*us* non guardades;
cavalgades pela sest' aqui
e cavalgades de noyt' outrossy,
e sospeytam que por mal cavalgades.

Mays rogo v*us* ora que mi creades
do que v*us* ora conselhar:
se queredes con as gentes estar,
Don [F]ernando, melhor ca no*n* estades,
sinher, for[ç]ade vosso cora[ç]on
e non cavalguedes tan sen razon,
siquer p*or* vossas bestas que matades.

86 Pero Garcia Burgalês

Song to a Man Who Never Stops Mounting

Don Fernando, though you scorn me,
it's as a friend I tell you now
that people are remarking how
you never cease from mounting horses;
you spend siesta mounting away,
and at night you mount the same,
and they suspect your mounting's sordid.

I beg you now to please consider
how I think this should be handled:
if you desire, Don Fernando,
to live in peace among your kinsmen,
then make an effort to curb you passion,
and mount less roughly and less rashly.
Think, at least, of the beasts you're killing.

87 Pero Garcia Burgalês

cantiga d'escarnho

Fernand' [E]scalho vi eu cantar ben,
que pouc*os* outr*os* vi cantar melhor,
e vy lhe sempre, mentre foy pastor,
muy boa voz, e vy o ca*n*tar ben;
mays ar direy v*us* p*er* que o perdeu:
ouve sabor de foder, e fodeu,
e perdeu todo o cantar poren.

Non se guardou de foder, e mal sen
fel' el, que non poderia peor;
e an lhas gentes p*or*en desamor,
p*er* bõa voz que perdeu co*n* mal sen,
voz de cabeça que xi lhi tolheu,
ca fodeu tanto que lh' enrouq*ue*ceu
a voz, e ora ja non canta ben.

Ca [D]on [F]ernando conteceu assy:
de mui bõa voz que soya aver,
soube a per avoleza perder,
ca fodeu moç', e non canta ja assy;
ar fodeu poys mui g*ra*[n]d' escudeyro*n*
e ficou ora, se D*eu*s mi perdon!
con a peyor voz que nunca vi.

E ora ainda mui g*ra*[n]d' infan[ç]o*n*
si quer foder, q*ue* nunca foy sazon
que mays quisesse foder, poylo eu vi.

87 Pero Garcia Burgalês

Song about a Man Who Once Sang Well

Fernando Escalho once sang well,
as very few have ever sung.
He had, as long as he was young,
a lovely voice that sang quite well,
and now I'll tell you how he lost it:
he liked to fuck and fucked a lot,
so that his singing went to hell.

In terms of fucking he was madder
than any man I have ever seen,
and people no longer pay him heed,
his voice not being the one he had.
He lost the high notes in his voice
from too much fucking – it went hoarse,
and now whatever he sings is bad.

This is how it all occurred:
Don Fernando had a good voice,
which he lost through too much vice;
he fucked a boy and his singing was hurt,
but then he fucked a grand old squire
and, God forgive me, thus acquired
the worst voice I have ever heard.

And now there's an even grander noble
he wants to fuck, and never so much
has he wanted to fuck, as far as I know.

descordo

Agora me quer' eu já espedir
da terra e das gentes que i son,
u mi Deus tanto de pesar mostrou;
e esforçar mui ben meu coraçon
e ar pensar de m'ir alhur guarir;
e a Deus gradesco por que m'en vou;

Ca, a meu grad', u m'eu daqui partir
con seus desejos, non me veeran
chorar, nen ir triste, por ben que eu
nunca presesse; nen me poderan
dizer que eu torto faç'en fogir
daqui, u me Deus tanto pesar deu;

Pero das terras averei soidade,
de que m' or' ei a partir, despagado;
e sempr' i tornará o meu cuidado
por quanto ben vi eu en elas já,
ca já por al nunca me veerá
nulh' ome ir triste nen desconortado.

E ben dig' a Deus, pois m'en vou, verdade:
se eu das gentes algun sabor avia
ou das terras en que guarecia,
por aquest' era tod' e non por al;
mais ora já nunca me será mal
por me partir delas e m' ir mia via.

Ca sei di mi
quanto sofri
e encobri
en esta terra de pesar.
Como perdi
e despendi,
vivend' aqui,
meus dias, posso-m' en queixar.

Discord

All I want now is to take my leave
from these people and this land,
where God has shown me grief on grief.
I'll do my best not to lose morale,
I'll start again, take up a new life
somewhere else. Thank God I can.

Once I'm gone, if I had my way,
I'd never be homesick for this place,
nor waste any tears recollecting
the few enjoyable moments I spent
(So much greater was the pain God dealt,
who can reproach my wish to forget?),

but I know that, yes, I will miss
the land I'm about to leave in anger:
my thoughts, at least, are sure to return
to whatever happiness I had there,
for in the new land where I'm going
no one will ever catch me in sadness.

Since I'm going, I'll tell God the truth:
except for the little bit of pleasure
I took in these people and this land,
I had good reason to complain.
Life will be better if I go away
to another people, another place.

Because I know
how much I cried
and held inside
in this land of bitterness.
How much I missed,
the time I lost
by staying on
and on, prolonging my distress.

E cuidarei
e pensarei
quant' aguardei
o ben, que nunca pud' achar.
Esforçar-m'ei
como guarrei,
e prenderei
conselh' agor' a meu cuidar.

Pe[n]sar
d'achar
logar,
provar
quer'eu, veer se poderei.
O sen
dalguen
ou ren
de ben
me valha, se o en mi ei!

Valer,
poder,
saber
dizer
ben me possa, que eu d' ir ei.
D' aver
poder,
prazer
prender
poss' eu, pois esto cobrarei.

Assi querrei
buscar,
viver
outra vida, que provarei,
e meu descord' acabarei!

With great regret
I will remember
how I waited
for the peace I could not find,
and I'll attempt
to take the nec-
essary steps
to quit my anxious state of mind.

Trying
to find
some peace
of mind
is hard, I'll do what I can.
May a friend's
good sense
or the good
in myself
help me, if such exists in man!

May wisdom,
my words,
my will
and my wits
uphold me now that I must go.
God grant
that I
might find
the satis-
faction I have never known.

Yes I
would like
to try
to live a life completely new,
so that my discord will be through.

sirventês

Quen viu o mundo qual o eu ja vi,
e viu as gentes que eran enton,
e viu aquestas que agora son,
Deus, quand'y cuyda, que pode cuydar?
Ca me sin'eu, per min, quando cuyd'y!
    Porque me non vou algur esterrar,
    se poderia mellor mund'achar?

Mundo tẽemos fals'e sen-sabor,
mundo sen Deus e en que ben non á,
e mundo tal que non corregerá:
ante, o vejo sempr'empeorar.
Quand'est' eu cat' e vej' end' o mellor,
    porque me [non vou algur esterrar,
    se poderia mellor mund'achar?]

U foy mesur', ou grãadez u jaz?
Verdad' u é? Quen á amigo leal?
Que fuy d'amor, ou trobar porque fal?
A gent'é trist' e sol non quer cantar!
Quand'est'eu cat' e quanto mal ss'i faz,
    porque me [non vou algur esterrar,
    se poderia mellor mund'achar?]

Viv' eu en tal mund', e faz-m'i viver
ũa dona que quero muy gran ben,
e muyt'á ja que m'en seu poder ten,
ben de-lo temp'u soýan amar:
oymays de min pode quenquer saber
    porque [me] non [vou algur esterrar,
    se poderia mellor mund'achar!]

Mays en tal mundo porque vay morar
ome de prez que s'én pod'alongar?

89 Martin Moxa

Song of How Come I Don't Go Away

Whoever has seen the world I've seen,
seen the people that lived back then
and seen the way they are today –
thinking about it, what can he think?
Crossing myself, I think 'God help us!'
How come I don't go away
to find another, better world?

Forsaking truth, the world turned sour,
with no more God or goodness in it,
a world so broken it can't be fixed,
and it gets worse each passing hour.
If this is really how I see it,
how come I don't go away
to find another, better world?

Where did grace and greatness flee?
Where went truth and the true friend?
What became of love and troubadours?
Why do people no longer sing?
When I consider all these things,
how come I don't go away
to find another, better world?

I live in such a world because
a lady I greatly love lives there.
I've been her slave since olden days,
back when love was still quite common.
This, if you want to know, explains
how come I don't go away
to find another, better world.

Why else would anyone keep on living
in such a world, if he could leave it?

90 Joam Zorro

cantiga d'amor

En Lixboa sôbre lo mar
barcas novas mandey lavrar,
ay mya senhor velida!

En Lixboa sôbre lo lez
barcas novas mandey fazer,
ay mya senhor velida!

Barcas novas mandey lavrar
e no mar as mandey deytar,
ay mya senhor velida!

Barcas novas mandey fazer
e no mar as mandey meter,
ay mya senhor velida!

90 Joam Zorro

Song of New Ships

On Lisbon's beach
I built new boats,
    oh lovely lady!

On Lisbon's shore
I built new ships,
    oh lovely lady!

I built new boats
and put them afloat,
    oh lovely lady!

I built new ships
and put them to sea,
    oh lovely lady!

91 Joam Zorro

cantiga d'amigo

El-rey de Portugale
barcas mandou lavrare,
e lá iran nas barcas migo
mya filha e noss' amigo.

El-rey portugueese
barcas mandou fazere,
e lá iran nas barcas migo
mya filha e noss' amigo.

Barcas mandou lavrare
e no mar as deytare,
e lá iran nas barcas migo
mya filha e noss' amigo.

Barcas mandou fazere
e no mar as metere,
e lá iran nas barcas migo
mya filha e noss' amigo.

91 Joam Zorro

Song about the Portuguese King's Boats

The king of Portugal
ordered boats made,
  and I, my daughter and our friend
  will set out together in them.

The Portuguese king
ordered boats built,
  and I, my daughter and our friend
  will set out together in them.

He ordered boats made
and moored in the bay,
  and I, my daughter and our friend
  will set out together in them.

He ordered boats built
and moored off the beach,
  and I, my daughter and our friend
  will set out together in them.

92 Joam Zorro

cantiga d'amigo

Jus' a lo mar e o rio
  eu namorada irey,
U el-rey arma navio,
  Amores, convusco m' irey.

Jus' a lo mar e o alto
  eu namorada irey,
U el-rey arma o barco,
  Amores, convusco m' irey.

U el-rey arma navio
  eu namorada irey,
pera levar a virgo,
  Amores, convusco m' irey.

U el-rey arma o barco
  eu namorada irey,
pera levar a d' algo,
  Amores, convusco m' irey.

92 Joam Zorro

Song of a Lady Who'll Go Down River

Down river to the sea
    I, full of love, will go.
Where the king rigs the ship:
    with you, my loves, I'll go.

Down river to the ocean
    I, full of love, will go.
Where the king rigs the boat:
    with you, my loves, I'll go.

Where the king rigs the ship
    (I, full of love, will go)
to carry a fair young virgin:
    with you, my loves, I'll go.

Where the king rigs the boat
    (I, full of love, will go)
to carry a virgin on board:
    with you, my loves, I'll go.

93 Joam Zorro

cantiga d'amigo

– Cabelos, los meus cabelos,
el-rey m' enviou por elos!
Madre, que lhis farey?
– Filha, dade-os a el-rey.

– Garcetas, las myas garcetas,
el-rey m' enviou por elas!
Madre, que lhis farey?
– Filha, dade-as a el-rey.

93 Joam Zorro

Song about a Request for Hair

– Mother, the king has declared
that he wants my hair. My hair!
What shall I do with it?
  – *Give it, daughter, to the king.*

– Mother, the king has sent word
that he wants my curls. My curls!
What shall I do with them?
  – *Give them, daughter, to the king.*

94 Joam Zorro

cantiga d'amigo

Pela ribeyra do rio salido
trebelhey, madre, con meu amigo:
amor ey migo
que non ouvesse!
fiz por amigo
que non fezesse!

Pela ribeyra do rio levado
trebelhey, madre, con meu amado:
amor ey migo
que non ouvesse!
fiz por amigo
que non fezesse!

94 Joam Zorro

Song of What I Shouldn't Have Done

There at the bend of the high-risen river
I frolicked, mother, with my lover.
    Would I didn't have
    the love that I have!
    With my lover I did
    what I shouldn't have!

There where the high-risen river bends
I frolicked, mother, with my friend.
    Would I didn't have
    the love that I have!
    With my lover I did
    what I shouldn't have!

95 Airas Nunez

cantiga d'amigo

Bailemos nós ja todas tres, ay amigas,
so aquestas avelaneyras frolidas,
e quen for velida como nós, velidas,
se amigo amar,
so aquestas avelaneyras frolidas
verrá baylar.

Bailemos nós ja todas tres, ay irmanas,
so aqueste ramo d'estas avelanas,
e quen for louçana como nós, louçanas,
se amigo amar,
so aqueste ramo d'estas avelanas
verrá baylar.

Por Deus, ay amigas, mentr'al non fazemos
so aqueste ramo frolido baylemos,
e quen ben parecer como nós parecemos,
se amigo amar,
so aqueste ramo, sol que nós bailemos,
verrá bailar.

95 Airas Nunez

Song of the Flowering Hazel Trees

Come on, you two, and dance with me,
under these flowering hazel trees,
and other girls who, like us, are pretty
      and truly in love
      will come dance with us
under these flowering hazel trees!

Why don't we dance as a threesome, friends,
under these hazel trees in flower?
And other girls who, like us, are fair
      and truly in love
      will come dance with us
under these hazel trees in flower!

Girls, since we have time on our hands,
let's dance here, under these hazels,
and other girls who, like us, are happy
      and truly in love
      will come dance with us
here where we dance, under these hazels!

96 Airas Nunez

sirventês

Porque no mundo mengou a verdade
punhey hum dia de a hyr buscar,
e hu por ela fuy preguntar
dis[s]eron todos: «Alhur la buscade,
ca de tal guisa se foy a perder
que non podemus én novas aver,
nen ja non anda na yrmaydade».

Nos moesteyros dos frades regrados
a demandey, e dis[s]eron-m'assy:
«Non busquedes vós a verdad'aqui
ca muytos anos avemos passados
que non morou nosco, per bõa fe,
. . . .
e d'al avemos mayores coidados».

E en Cistel, hu verdade soya
sempre morar, dis[s]eron-me que non
morava hy avya gran sazon,
nen frade d'y ja a non conhocia;
nen o abbade outrosy no estar
sol non queria que foss'y pousar
e anda ja fora da badia.

En Ssantyago, seend'albergado
en mha pousada, chegaron rromeus;
preguntey-os e dis[s]eron: «Par Deus,
muyto levade-lo caminh'errado,
ca se verdade quiserdes achar
outro caminho conven a buscar,
ca non saben aqui d'ela mandado».

96 Airas Nunez

Song in Search of Truth

Since truth was missing from the world
I decided to go and look for her,
but everywhere I took my search
I was told, 'Take a different way,
for she's so long gone from our midst
she doesn't even come for visits
nor any longer send us word.'

In monasteries that keep the Rule
I asked for her, and the monks replied:
'To ask us is to waste your time,
as we haven't seen a sign of truth
in recent years, and we don't know
or worry about where she is now.
We've got better things to do.'

And in Cistercium, where I was sure
I'd find the truth, they said she'd left
a while ago. No friar confessed
to having ever worshipped her,
and the abbot said, 'I'd never allow
her back, not even in the guest house.
She's left for good and can't return.'

In Santiago, at the hospice
where I and other pilgrims stayed,
I told my quest. 'For God's sake,'
they said, 'you couldn't be more lost!
If truth is really your aspiration,
you'd better try in other places,
for by here her path doesn't cross.'

97 Airas Nunez

cantiga d'amor

Que muyto m'eu pago d'este verão
por estes rramos e por estas flores,
e polas aves que cantan d'amores,
por que ando hy led'e sen cuydado;
e assy faz tod'omen namorado:
sempre y anda led'e muy loução.

Cand'eu passo per algũas rribeiras,
so bõas arvores, per bõos prados,
se cantan hy passaros namorados
log'eu con amores hy vou cantando,
e log'aly d'amores vou trobando,
e faço cantares en mil maneyras.

Ey eu gran viç[o] e grand'alegria
quando mhas aves cantan no estyo.

97 Airas Nunez

Song of Love in the Summer

How very much I love this summer,
its flowers, trees and sky above,
and all the birds that sing of love,
because I feel at peace and happy
and even handsome – that's what happens
whenever anyone loves another.

When I walk on certain shores,
under branches and through pastures,
if I hear birds sing with passion
then with love and all my heart
and all I know of troubadour art
I make up songs of every sort.

I feel happy, all of a sudden,
when I hear birds sing in summer.

cantiga d'amigo

– Digades, filha, mya filha velida,
porque tardastes na fontana fria.
Os amores ey.

– Digades, filha, mya filha louçana,
porque tardastes na fria fontana.
Os amores ey.

– Tardey, mya madre, na fontana fria,
cervos do monte a áugua volvian.
Os amores ey.

– Tardey, mya madre, na fria fontana,
cervos do monte volvian a áugua.
Os amores ey.

– Mentir, mya filha, mentir por amigo,
nunca vi cervo que volvess'o rio.
Os amores ey.

– Mentir, mya filha, mentir por amado,
nunca vi cervo que volvess'o alto.
Os amores ey.

98 Pero Meogo

Song about a Girl Back from the Spring

Tell me, daughter, fair and pretty,
why you tarried at the cold spring.
I'm very in love.

Tell me, daughter, pretty and fair,
why at the cold spring you tarried.
I'm very in love.

I tarried, mother, at the cold spring,
as mountain stags made the waters stir.
I'm very in love.

At the cold spring, mother, I tarried,
as mountain stags made the waters wave.
I'm very in love.

You're lying, daughter, lying for your friend:
I've never seen a stag stir up the stream.
I'm very in love.

You're lying, daughter, lying for your lover:
I've never seen a stag stir up the river.
I'm very in love.

99 Pero Meogo

cantiga d'amigo

[Levou-s'a louçana,] levou-s'a velida:
vay lavar cabelos, na fontana fria.
Leda dos amores, dos amores leda.

[Levou-s'a velida,] levou-s'a louçana:
vay lavar cabelos, na fria fontana.
Leda dos amores, dos amores leda.

Vay lavar cabelos, na fontana fria:
passou seu amigo, que lhi ben queria.
Leda dos amores, dos amores leda.

Vay lavar cabelos, na fria fontana:
passa seu amigo, que a muyt'amava.
Leda dos amores, dos amores leda.

Passa seu amigo, que lhi ben queria:
o cervo do monte a áugua volvia.
Leda dos amores, dos amores leda.

Passa seu amigo, que a muyt'amava:
o cervo do monte volvia a áugua.
Leda dos amores, dos amores leda.

99 Pero Meogo

Song about a Girl at a Spring

She wakes up fresh, she wakes up fair:
she goes to the spring to wash her hair.
    Happily in love, in love she's happy.

She wakes up fair, she wakes up fresh:
she goes to the spring to wash her face.
    Happily in love, in love she's happy.

She goes to the spring to wash her hair:
her adoring boyfriend meets her there.
    Happily in love, in love she's happy.

She goes to the spring to wash her face:
there she meets her enamoured friend.
    Happily in love, in love she's happy.

Her adoring boyfriend meets her there:
a mountain stag makes the waters stir.
    Happily in love, in love she's happy.

There she meets her enamoured friend:
a mountain stag makes the waters wave.
    Happily in love, in love she's happy.

cantiga d'amigo

Levantou-s' a velida,
levantou-s' alva
e vai lavar camisas
eno alto:
vai-las lavar alva.

Levantou-s' a louçãa,
levantou-s' alva
e vai lavar delgadas
eno alto:
vai-las lavar alva.

[E] vai lavar camisas;
levantou-s' alva;
o vento lh'as desvia
eno alto:
vai-las lavar alva.

E vai lavar delgadas;
levantou-s' alva;
o vento lh'as levava
eno alto:
vai-las lavar alva.

O vento lh'as desvia;
levantou-s' alva;
meteu-s' alva en ira
eno alto:
vai-las lavar alva.

O vento lh'as levava;
levantou-s' alva;
meteu-s' alva en sanha
eno alto:
vai-las lavar alva.

Song of Clean Shirts

She wakes up lovely
    bright and early
and goes to wash shirts
    at the stream.
    She'll wash them bright and clean.

She wakes up pretty
    bright and early
and washes chemises
    at the stream.
    She'll wash them bright and clean.

She goes to wash shirts
    bright and early;
they're strewn by the wind
    at the stream.
    She'll wash them bright and clean.

She washes chemises
    bright and early;
they're strewn by the breeze
    at the stream.
    She'll wash them bright and clean.

They're strewn by the wind
    bright and early;
she becomes livid
    at the stream.
    She'll wash them bright and clean.

They're strewn by the breeze
    bright and early;
she begins seething
    at the stream.
    She'll wash them bright and clean.

cantiga d'amigo

– Ai flores, ai flores do verde pĩo,
se sabedes novas do meu amigo?
ai, Deus, e u é?

Ai flores, ai flores do verde ramo,
se sabedes novas do meu amado?
ai, Deus, e u é?

Se sabedes novas do meu amigo,
aquel que mentiu do que pôs comigo?
ai, Deus, e u é?

Se sabedes novas do meu amado
aquel que mentiu do que mi á jurado?
ai, Deus, e u é?

– Vós me preguntades polo voss' amigo?
E eu ben vos digo que é sã' e vivo:
ai, Deus, e u é?

Vós me preguntades polo voss' amado?
E eu ben vos digo que é viv' e são:
ai, Deus, e u é?

E eu ben vos digo que é sã' e vivo
e seerá vosc' ant' o prazo saido:
ai, Deus, e u é?

E eu ben vos digo que é viv' e são
e s[e]erá vosc' ant' o prazo passado:
ai, Deus, e u é?

Song of the Flower of the Green Pine

Flower of the green pine, oh flower,
do you have news of my lover?
    Oh God, and where is he?

Oh flower, flower of the green branch,
do you have news of my friend?
    Oh God, and where is he?

Do you have news of my lover,
who has proved himself a liar?
    Oh God, and where is he?

Do you have news of my friend,
who did not come when he said?
    Oh God, and where is he?

You ask me about your lover?
I tell you he's well, he's coming.
    Oh God, and where is he?

You ask me about your friend?
I tell you he's coming, he's well.
    Oh God, and where is he?

I tell you he's well, he's coming,
he'll keep his word – take comfort.
    Oh God, and where is he?

I tell you he's coming, he's well,
he'll be here – patience! – in a while.
    Oh God, and where is he?

cantiga d'amigo

– En grave dia, senhor, que vos oí
falar e vos viron estes olhos meus!
– Dized', amigo, que poss'eu fazer i,
en aqueste feito, se vos valha Deus.
– Faredes mesura contra mi, senhor?
– Farei, amigo, fazend'eu o melhor.

– U vos en tal ponto eu oí falar,
senhor, que non pudi depois ben aver.
– Amigo, quero-vos ora preguntar
que mi digades o que poss'i fazer.
– Faredes mesura contra mi, senhor?
– Farei, amigo, fazend'eu o melhor.

– Des que vos vi e vos oí falar, [non]
vi prazer, senhor, nen dormi, nen folguei.
– Amigo, dizede, se Deus vos perdon,
o que eu i faça, ca eu non o sei.
– Faredes mesura contra mi, senhor?
– Farei, amigo, fazend'eu o melhor.

Song of a Lover Asking Favour

– On a dreadful day, dear lady, I heard
you speak and first laid eyes on you.
– Tell me, friend, since you are hurting,
what, by God's grace, I can do?
– Will you show me your favour, lady?
– Yes, my friend, as far as I'm able.

– On the day I heard you speak,
dear lady, I lost all happiness.
– Friend, in earnest I make this plea:
tell me what I can do to help.
– Will you show me your favour, lady?
– Yes, my friend, as far as I'm able.

– Seeing and hearing you speak, dear lady,
robbed me of pleasure, peace and sleep.
– Then tell me, friend, God allowing,
what I can do, for I've no idea.
– Will you show me your favour, lady?
– Yes, my friend, as far as I'm able.

cantiga d'escarnho

U noutro dia seve Don Foan,
a mi começou gran noj' a crecer
de muitas cousas que lh' oí dizer.
Diss' el: – Ir-m'-ei, ca já se deitar an.
    E dix' eu: – Boa ventura ajades,
    por que vos ides e me leixades.

E muit' enfadado de seu parlar,
sêvi gran peça, se mi valha Deus,
e tosquiavan estes olhos meus.
E quand' el disse: – Ir-me quer' eu deitar,
    e dix' eu: – Bõa ventura ajades,
    por que vos ides e me leixades.

El seve muit' e diss' e parfiou,
e a min creceu gran nojo poren,
e non soub' el se x' era mal, se ben.
E quand' el disse: – Já m' eu deitar vou,
    Dixi-lh' eu: – Bõa ventura ajades,
    por que vos ides e me leixades.

103 Dinis, King of Portugal

Song about a Mr So-and-So

Mr So-and-so, the other evening,
talked so much I thought he'd keep me
up all night, till finally he said,
'I'm going home, it's time for bed,'
        and I said, 'Have a good night's sleep,
        now that you're going to leave me in peace.'

I got so sick of having to listen
to the guy go on – God be my witness –
I couldn't keep my eyelids open,
and when he said, 'I'm going home,'
        then I said, 'Have a good night's sleep,
        now that you're going to leave me in peace.'

He chattered on for such a long time
I thought I was going to lose my mind,
and he thought he was being interesting!
And when he said, 'I'm turning in,'
        then I said, 'Have a good night's sleep,
        now that you're going to leave me in peace.'

cantiga d'amor

Quer' eu en maneyra de proençal
fazer agora hun cantar d' amor
e querrey muyt' i loar mha senhor,
a que prez nen fremusura non fal,
nen bondade, e mays vos direy en:
tanto a fez Deus comprida de ben
que mays que todas las do mundo val.

Ca mha senhor quiso Deus fazer tal
quando a fez, que a fez sabedor
de todo ben e de mui gran valor
e con tod[o] est' é mui comunal,
aly hu deve; er den-lhi bon sen
e des y non lhi fez pouco de ben,
quando non quis que lh' outra foss' igual.

Ca en mha senhor nunca Deus pôs mal,
mays pôs hi prez e beldad' e loor
e falar mui ben e riir melhor
que outra molher; des y é leal
muyt', e por esto non sey oj' eu quen
possa compridamente no seu ben
falar, ca non á, tra-lo seu ben, al.

Song in Provençal Style

In Provençal style I'd like
to make a song of love
in order to praise my lady,
whose looks and talents lack
in nothing. God granted her
so much in fact that she's
the fairest in the land.

So that she'd be the best
among all women, He made her
wise and full of merit,
yet also frank and friendly.
He gave her common sense
and other gifts that raised
her far above the rest.

Yes God took every care
to make my lady pretty,
clever, and gentle in speech
like no one else, and very
loyal. I really can't think
of another lady worth speaking
about, for who could compare?

cantiga d'amor

Proençaes soen mui ben trobar
e dizen eles que é con amor,
mays os que trobam no tempo da flor
e non en outro sey eu ben que non
am tam gran coyta no seu coraçon
qual m' eu por mha senhor vejo levar.

Pero que troban e saben loar
sas senhores o mays e o melhor
que eles poden, sõo sabedor
que os que troban, quand' a frol sazon
á e non ante, se Deus mi perdon,
non an tal coyta qual eu ey sen par.

Ca os que troban e que ss' alegrar
van eno tempo que ten a color
a frol consigu' e, tanto que se fôr
aquel tempo, logu' en trobar razon
non an, non viven [en] qual perdiçon
oj' eu vyvo, que poys m' á de matar.

105 Dinis, King of Portugal

Song about the Provençal Poets

The Provençal poets make fine verses,
and they say they do it with love,
but poets who make their verses
only in the time of flowers
know nothing of the painful poem
my heart bears for my lady.

I know they know how to praise
the ladies they love in song,
and how ardently they sing!
But those who only in Spring
sing praises can never know
the torment my heart sings.

Those who rejoice and make poems
when the flower is full with colour
and, once the season is over,
forget their calling as poets,
don't know the hell I am living,
this love that keeps on killing.

cantiga d'amor

Hun tal home sey eu, ay ben talhada,
que por vós ten a sa morte chegada;
vede q[u]em é e seed' en nenbrada;
eu, mha dona.

Hun tal home sey [eu] que preto sente
de ssy morte [chegada] certamente;
vede que[m] é e venha-vos en mente;
eu, mha dona.

Hun tal home sey [eu]; aquest' oyde:
que por vós morr' e vó-lo [en] partide,
vede que[m] é [e] non xe vos obride;
eu, mha dona.

106 Dinis, King of Portugal

Song about a Man I Know

I know a man, O beloved so fair,
whose death is at hand, your hand;
open your eyes so as to remember
    me, dear lady.

I know a man whose fate is decided,
whose death is doubtless close by;
open your eyes and recall to mind
    me, dear lady.

I know a man – hear his distress! –
whose life you kill with your distance;
open your eyes so as not to forget
    me, dear lady.

cantiga d'amor

Senhor fremosa, vejo-vos queixar
porque vos am', e no meu coraçon
ey muy gram pesar, se Deus mi perdon,
porque vej' end' a vós aver pesar
e queria-m' en de grado quytar,
mays non posso forçar o coraçon,

Que mi forçou meu saber e meu sen,
des i meteu-me no vosso poder
e do pesar que vos eu vej' aver
par Deus, senhor, a min pesa muyt' en
e partir-m' ia de vos querer ben,
mays tolhe-m' end' o coraçon poder,

Que me forçou de tal guisa, senhor,
que sen, nen força non ey já de mi
e do pesar que vós tomades hy
tom' eu pesar, que non posso mayor,
e queria non vos aver amor,
mays o coraçon pode mays ca mi.

107 Dinis, King of Portugal

Song for a Vexed Lady

Fair lady, I know you complain
my love is a nuisance. Believe me,
I regret the vexation you feel
because of this passion I harbour,
and I would love to be free of it,
but I cannot force this heart

That forced away sense and reason,
and forced me into your power.
The vexation you feel, God knows,
is vexing for my part,
and I'd quit this love tomorrow
if I could, but I have a heart

That forced me, fair lady, to quit
my sense and reason. I would do
anything to cure your vexation
were it not useless to try;
I'd love to stop this love,
but my heart is stronger than I.

pastorela

Ũa pastor ben talhada
cuidava en seu amigo
e estava, ben vos digo,
per quant'eu vi, mui coitada,
e diss': «Oimais non é nada
de fiar per namorado
nunca molher namorada,
poisque mi o meu á errado.»

Ela tragia na mão
um papagai mui fremoso,
cantando mui saboroso,
ca entrava o verão,
e diss': «Amigo loução,
que faria per amores,
pois m'errastes tan en vão?»
E caeu antr'ũas flores.

Ũa gran peça do dia
jouv'ali, que non falava,
e a vezes acordava,
e a vezes esmorecia,
e diss': «Ai santa Maria,
que será de min agora?»
E o papagai dizia:
«Bem, por quant'eu sei, senhora.»

«Se me queres dar guarida»
diss'a pastor, «di verdade,
papagai, por caridade,
ca morte m'é esta vida»
Diss'el: «Senhor [mui] comprida
de ben, e non vos queixedes,
ca o que vos á servida
erged'olho e vee-lo-edes.»

Pastoral Song

A pretty shepherd girl
was thinking of her lover,
and I could tell by looking
that she was feeling grieved,
and she said, 'Never again
should a girl in love believe
what a man in love claims,
for my man abandoned me.'

In her hand she carried
a bright and beautiful parrot,
whose singing was quite pleasant,
for Spring was in the air,
and she asked, 'How recover
my dear and handsome lover
who left me for no reason?'
And she fell into the flowers.

For a good part of the day
she lay without a word,
and sometimes she would stir,
and sometimes she would faint,
and she said, 'Holy Mary,
what will become of me now?'
And the parrot answered, 'Lady,
you'll prosper, as far as I know.'

'If you wish to help me,
parrot, for goodness' sake
be honest,' the shepherdess said,
'as I'm in a living hell.'
And he said, 'Lovely lady,
have some faith and courage:
just lift your eyes and see
the loyal one who serves you.'

109 Estevan Coelho

cantiga d'amigo

Sedia la fremosa seu sirgo torcendo,
sa voz manselinha fremoso dizendo
cantigas d'amigo.

Sedia la fremosa seu sirgo lavrando,
sa voz manselinha fremoso cantando
cantigas d'amigo.

– Par Deus de Cruz, dona, sei eu que avedes
amor mui coitado que tan ben dizedes
cantigas d'amigo.

Par Deus de Cruz, dona, sei [eu] que andades
d'amor mui coitada que tan ben cantades
cantigas d'amigo.

– Avuitor comestes, que adevinhades.

109 Estevan Coelho

Song of a Girl Spinning Silk

While spinning silk a beautiful girl
in a soft, beautiful voice was singing
    songs of love.

While spinning silk a beautiful woman
in a soft, beautiful voice was humming
    songs of love.

– *By God on the cross, lady, I think there's*
someone for whom you so well sing these
    songs of love.

By God on the cross, lady, there must be
someone for whom you so well hum these
    songs of love.

– How did you guess? By eating some vulture?

cantiga d'amigo

Vayamos, irmana, vayamos dormir
nas rrybas do lago, hu eu andar vy
a las aves, meu amigo.

Vaiamos, hirmana, vaiamos folgar
nas rribas do lago, hu eu vi andar
a las aves, meu amigo.

Enas rribas do lago, hu eu andar vi,
seu arco na maão as aves ferir,
a las aves, meu amigo.

Enas rribas do lago, hu eu vi andar,
seu arco na mano a las aves tirar,
a las aves, meu [amigo].

Seu arco na mano as aves ferir,
e las que cantavan leixa-las guarir,
a las aves, meu [amigo].

Seu arco na mano a las aves tyrar,
e las que cantavam non-nas quer matar,
a las aves, m[eu amigo].

110 Fernand'Esquio

Song about a Girl's Beloved Who Hunts

Come with me, sister, and we'll go sit
alongside the lake where I have seen
    my beloved hunting for birds.

Come with me, sister, and we will walk
alongside the lake where I have watched
    my beloved hunting for birds.

Alongside the lake where I have seen
his arrows shooting birds in the trees,
    my beloved hunting for birds.

Alongside the lake where I have watched
his arrows shooting birds on the water,
    my beloved hunting for birds.

His arrows shooting birds in the trees,
but he never aims at birds that sing,
    my beloved hunting for birds.

His arrows shooting birds on the water,
but he never aims at birds that warble,
    my beloved hunting for birds.

111 Fernand'Esquio

cantiga d'escarnho

A hũu frade dizen escaralhado
e faz pecado quen lh'o vay dizer
ca, pois el ssab'arreytar de foder,
cuyd'eu que gaj'é de piss'arreitado;
e, poys emprenha estas con que jaz
e faze filhos e filhas assaz,
ante lhe digu'eu ben encaralhado.

Escaralhado nunca eu diria,
mays que traje ant'[o] caralho arreyte,
ao que tantas molheres de leyte
ten ca lhe pariron tres en hũu dia
e outras muytas prenhadas que ten;
e atal frade cuyd'eu que muy ben
encaralhado per esto sseria.

Escaralhado non pode sseer
o que tantas filhas fez en Marinha
e que ten ora outra pastorinha
prenhe que ora quer encaecer
e outras muytas molheres que fode;
e atal frade bem cuyd'eu que pode
encaralhado per esto sseer.

111 Fernand'Esquio

Song about a Friar Said to be Impotent

A friar they say is impotent
really doesn't fit the case,
for he knows how to fornicate,
and so his cock's quite competent;
he gets the girls he lies with pregnant,
making sons and daughters aplenty,
so I would say he's well equipped.

Instead of 'impotent' I would say
his cock is stiff and ready to fuck,
for look at his women giving suck;
three gave birth on the same day,
and he's got others now expecting,
so that the friar, by my reckoning,
is well equipped, with power to stay.

'Impotent' is not the word
for one who's given so many children
to Marinha, and now a different
girl he fucks will soon give birth,
and there are many others he fucks;
I'm sure that such a friar must
be equipped with a cock that works.

cantiga d'amor

Faz-m'agora por ssy morrer
e tras-me muy coitado
mha ssenhor do bom parecer
e do cos bem talhado;
a por que ey mort' a prender
come çervo lançado,
que ssy vay do mund'a perder
da companha das cervas.

E mal dia non ensandecy
e pasesse das hervas
e non viss'u primeyro vi,
a muy fremosinha d'Elvas.

Oymais a morrer me conven,
ca tan coytado sejo
pola mha ssenhor do bom sem,
que am'e que desejo,
a que me parec'er tan ben
cada que a eu vejo,
que semelha rrosa que ven,
quando sal d'antr'as rrelvas.

E mal dia non ensandecy
[e pacesse das hervas
e non viss', u primeyro vi,
a muy fremosinha d'Elvas].

Song to a Lady from Elvas

My lady's making me perish
from grief born of my passion
for her, who is so pleasant,
whose body is finely fashioned,
and for whom I'm facing death,
like a stag when it is banished
from the does and all the rest
that in life it loved so well.
    If only on that day I'd been
    deranged or under a spell
    so that I never would have seen
    that lovely lady from Elvas.

I wish my life were through,
because I'm sick of grieving
for this fine lady whom
I want and love sincerely.
Her beauty is so true
that every time I see her
I think of roses blooming
amidst the grass in dells.
    If only on that day I'd been
    deranged or under a spell
    so that I never would have seen
    that lovely lady from Elvas.

113 Afonso Sanchez and Vasco Martins

cantiga d'escarnho

– Vaasco Martĩiz, pois vos trabalhades
e trabalhastes de trobar d'amor,
de que agora, par Nostro Senhor,
quero saber de vós que mi o digades;
e dizede-mi-o, ca ben vos estará:
pois vos esta, por que trobastes, já
morreu, par Deus, por quen [ora] trobades?

– Afonso Sánchez, vós [me] preguntades
e quero-vos eu fazer sabedor:
eu trobo e trobei pola melhor
das que Deus fez – esto ben o creades;
esta do coraçon non me salrá,
e atenderei seu ben se mi o fará;
e vós al de min saber non queirades.

– Vaasco Martĩiz, vós non respondedes,
nen er entendo, assi veja prazer,
por que trobades, ca ouvi dizer
que aquela por que trobad' avedes
e que amastes vós mais d' outra ren,
que vos morreu á gran temp' e poren
pola mort' [ora] trobar non devedes.

– Afonso Sánchez, pois non entendedes
en qual guisa vos eu fui responder,
a min en culpa non deven poer,
mais a vós, se o saber non podedes:
eu trobo pola que m'en poder ten
e vence todas de parecer ben,
pois viva é, ca non como dizedes.

– Vaasco Martĩiz, pois vos morreu por quen
sempre trobastes, maravilho-m' en,
pois vos morreu, como [vós] non morredes.

113 Afonso Sanchez and Vasco Martins

Song about a Living Dead Lady

– Vasco Martins, you who strive
as always, making troubadour songs
of love, I'd like to know by God
(if you don't mind me asking) why
you make them still, seeing as the lady
for whom you've sung and sing is dead?

– Afonso Sanchez, since you ask,
I'll try my best to tell you why.
My singing was and is for the finest
of God's creatures, be sure of that;
and in my heart she will remain,
for I still hope to gain her favour.

– Vasco Martins, you haven't answered
and I don't understand, so please,
tell me why your songs entreat
this lady you loved above all others
but who has already passed away:
why do you sing to a dead lady?

– Afonso Sanchez, if you can't catch
my meaning which I think was plain,
then I am not the one to blame
but you yourself, who didn't grasp.
I sing for one I can't betray,
who is alive and not as you say.

– Vasco Martins, since the lady
for whom you've always sung is dead,
I marvel you don't likewise die.

– Afonso Sánchez, vós sabede ben
que viva é e comprida de sen
a por que trob' e [vós] sabê-lo-edes.

– Afonso Sanchez, you know right well
that every troubadour song I've made
is for a lady who is quite alive.

Notes to the Poems

The original manuscript source(s) for each *cantiga* is followed by the source for the edited version reproduced here. Numbers, unless preceded by a p. or pp., refer to texts rather than pages. See the *Introduction* for descriptions of the manuscript sources. See the *Bibliography* for complete references to the published editions.

KEY TO ABBREVIATIONS

(for the profane *cantigas*:)

A = Songbook of the Ajuda Palace Library (in Lisbon)
B = Songbook of the National Library (in Lisbon)
R = Vindel Manuscript
V = Songbook of the Vatican Library
CM = Carolina Michaëlis de Vasconcelos, *Cancioneiro da Ajuda.*
JN[1] = José Joaquim Nunes, *Cantigas de Amigo.*
JN[2] = José Joaquim Nunes, *Cantigas de Amor.*
RL = Rodrigues Lapa, *Cantigas d'escarnho e de mal dizer*, Vigo 1970. (Text numbers from this revised and enlarged edition vary from those of the original, 1965 edition.)

(for the *Songs in Praise of Holy Mary*, Nos.46-48:)

E = Marian Songbook (w/415 *cantigas*) of the Escorial Monastery
T = Marian Songbook (w/193 *cantigas*) of the Escorial Monastery
To = Marian Songbook of Toledo, now in the National Library of Madrid.
WM = Walter Mettmann, ed., *Cantigas de Santa Maria.*

1. B 456; Vasconcelos, pp.17-18.

The verses in the ms. were arranged thus:

Ai eu, coitada, como vivo
em gram cuidado por meu amigo
que ei alongado! Muito me tarda
o meu amigo na Guarda!

etc.

Heading immediately before text attributes it to 'King Alfonso of León', which could refer to Alfonso IX, King of León from 1188-1230, or to Alfonso X, King of León and Castile from 1252-1284. But the preceding page identifies Sancho I (ruled Portugal from 1185-1211) as the author. CM (v.II, pp.593-595) provides convincing arguments for attributing the *cantiga* to Sancho I, who enlarged and fortified Guarda, the highest town in Portugal, at the end of the twelfth century. Pellegrini, pp.78-93, argues that Alfonso X is the probable author.

The notions of desire (1st stanza) and worry (2nd stanza) appear in reverse order in the original. The refrain is literally 'My friend is tarrying a long time in Guarda!'

2. A 35, B 150; CM 35.

The third and fourth lines of the second stanza literally read 'and of whom God made him see things that caused him to die with bitterness'. In the fourth lines of the first and third stanzas, the hypothetical lover also actually dies.

3. A 38; Bertolucci, *Martin Soares* 5.

Difficult *cantiga* to transcribe and to interpret. There is doubt about the author (hence Bertolucci's inclusion of the text in her edition of Martin Soarez's *cantigas*), but most scholars now agree with CM in attributing it to Pai Soarez. Some consider this to be a *cantiga d'escarnho*.

The 'red and white' of verse four might refer to the woman's make-up or clothing. Paio Moniz was the father of Maria Pais Ribeirinha, who was mistress to Sancho I and is doubtless the same woman referred to here.

4. B 48; CM 332.

Monte-Maior was a fortified town built in the eleventh century to defend Coimbra against the Moors. The poet's half-sisters, and very possibly his wife, were in the town in 1213, when it was besieged by King Afonso II (the poet's half-brother), who contested the will that had assigned the town's castle and other feudal properties to his sisters. This, Gil Sanchez's only surviving *cantiga*, was probably written in or about that year.

The repeated lines suggest a popular, primitive model, yet the refrain is unusually long and complex.

5. B 39a [unnumbered, falls between B 39 and 40]; CM 323.

6. B 632, V 233; JN[1] 66.

7. B 627, V 228; JN[1] 61.

Fourth stanza: 'I'll kill myself, if you tell me that you're able to live without me.'

8. B 1252, V 857; JN[1] 464.

Four of Lopo's *cantigas d'amigo* mention a St Eleutherius, of which there are at least three, all of them martyrs. This is no doubt the one with a shrine in Galicia. According to JN[1], a pilgrimage is made there on 20 May in honour of the saint, who is invoked to fight against rabies.

9. B 1366, V 974; Bertolucci, *Martin Soares* 41.

In one of the poet's other three satires against Lopo, we're told that listeners would give the jongleur money or a present to be spared his playing the *cítola*, a kind of guitar, and then a further remuneration so that he would quit singing.

10. A 46, B 158; Bertolucci, *Martin Soares* 14.

The repeating, rhetorical questioning of the last two stanzas is typical of certain Provençal poets, particularly Uc de Saint Circ, whose 'Tres enemics e dos mals seignors ai' contains verses that were virtually translated by Soares.

11. B 1579, V 1111; RL 37.

Second stanza, final line: 'and I remained young'.

12. B 1617, V 1150; RL 52.

Attributed in B to Pero Viviaez.

13. B 1575; RL 333.

Last stanza, line 1: 'And you'd be able – I know – '.

14. V 592-593; RL 388.

15. B 374; RL 399.

16. B 918, V 505; JN[1] 260.

First stanza, line 1: 'I'm miserable, by God,'; lines 4-5: 'O hair, I won't tie you with [my] silk ribbon.' Second stanza, line 3: '...detained by the king'; the bonnets in line 4 come from Estela, a city in Navarre. The 'sisters' of the third stanza are female friends, while the 'dear friends' of the final stanza are identified as 'maidens'.

17. B 641, V 242; Tavani, *Poesia del Duecento*, pp.267-68.

Many critics consider these verses to be modelled after the Provençal *alba*, in which dawn (the *alba*) breaks and the woman laments the parting of her lover, with whom she has spent the night. Although the first half line of this *cantiga* might imply such a scenario, the rest of the song suggests that the lover is not present – the woman is merely recalling the love they once had. 'Rise up!', as if she would resurrect that love.

Refrain is literally 'Happy I go'. Line 1 of the second stanza, rather than substituting 'clear' for 'cold', merely changes the word order of line 1 of the first stanza.

18. B 645, V 246; JN[1] 79.

Final stanza, line 2: 'whom it was my misfortune to meet'.

19. B 829, V 415; Reali, 'Pedr'Eanes Solaz' 6.

'Dellaly dare, way dellaly dare' is offered in place of the original gibberish 'lelia doura, edoi lelia doura'. Nonsense refrains were common in ancient French songs and are still found in modern Galician folk music.

Literal rendering, with original nonsense words:

I, who am fair, could not sleep,
lelia doura,
and my friend was coming,
edoi lelia doura.

I couldn't sleep and I worried,
lelia doura,
and my friend was arriving,
edoi lelia doura.

My friend was coming,
lelia doura,
and spoke so well of love,
edoi lelia doura.

My friend was arriving,
lelia doura,
and sang so well of love,
edoi lelia doura.

Friend, I greatly longed,
lelia doura,
to have you here with me,
edoi lelia doura.

Beloved, I greatly longed,
lelia doura,
to have you at my side,
edoi lelia doura.

Leli, leli, by God, leli,
lelia doura,
I know who doesn't say leli,
edoi lelia doura.

I know who doesn't say leli,
lelia doura,
it's the devil who doesn't say leli,
edoi lelia doura.

20. A 292, B 983, V 570; Panunzio 5.

Third stanza, line 1: 'Ah me, miserable and unhappy!'

21. A 289, B 980, V 567; Panunzio 2.

This *cantiga* is built on the technique of *mozdobre*, in which words are repeated in different inflections. (Cf. Section 4, Chapters 5 and 6, of the *Arte de Trobar [Art of Troubadour Poetry]*, found in the opening folios of B.)

Final stanza, line 2: 'the one who never asked me'; line 5: 'And this is why I suffer'.

22. B 1642, V 1176; Panunzio 17, w/modified strophic division and with modified 4th verse as per Roncaglia, p.20.

Maria Perez Balteira was a singer and dancer, and presumably a courtesan, in the courts of Ferdinand III and Alfonso X. Her sexual promiscuity gave rise to a number of satiric *cantigas* by half a dozen troubadours, who became all the more virulent after she 'got religion' and went on a crusade to the Holy Land.

First stanza, line 5: 'but they steal them from her, wherever [*or* whenever] she goes to lie down'.

23. B 1635, V 1169; Panunzio 10.

Nobles would compensate visiting troubadours and jongleurs with a *don* [gift] that might consist of money, food, clothes or other goods. Pero da Ponte was evidently not happy with the *don* he received from the Spanish aristocrat named in the first line. Faro refers to Alfaro, a town on the Ebro River in northern Spain.

Second stanza, lines 1-2: 'Your cloths are expensive for us,/ so that no one would dare ask for them'; line 4: 'they're cheap [shabby] for that reason'.

24. B 1643, V 1177; Panunzio 18.

'Rich man', written as one word (*rico ome* = *ricome*), designated a noble rank rather than an elevated economic status, which usually but not always came with the rank.

The translation assumes a copyist's error – *daria* instead of *dariam* – in the final line of the first stanza. Not assuming an error, the last two lines of the stanza would translate: 'For they all said he wouldn't/ pay anything for him[self?]'. Second stanza, first 4 lines: 'Anyone could tell you/ the truth about this rich man:/ since he never even learned a trade,/ who wound want to waste [their money] on him?'

25. B 1655, V 1189; Panunzio 29, with modified strophic division.

As the note to this *cantiga* in the Songbooks indicates, the lampoon is in fact against Don Manuel, the brother of Alfonso X. Some scholars believe that the second stanza mentioned in the note is missing, but the clues in the final lines clearly point to Don Manuel, so that we may consider them the closure to the second stanza.

First stanza, line 4: 'meanness' rather than 'ineptness'; sixth line: 'lord' rather than 'dumb ass'.

26. A 229, B 419, V 30; CM 229.

First stanza, line 3: 'because I see myself act madly'. Refrain, line 2: 'make me act this way'.

27. B 746, V 348; JN[1] 181.

First stanza, line 1 (and again in line 2 of the second stanza): 'women' [female friends, companions] rather than 'sisters'; fifth line: 'another crazy thing' rather than 'something else'.

28. B 749, V 352; JN[1] 184.

Refrain: 'for we'll say many things to each other/ that we would not say in front of you'.

29. B 754, V 357; JN[1] 189.

30. B 750, V 353; JN[1] 185.

Last stanza, line 4: 'and may he die, if that's his pleasure'.

31. A 234, B 424, V 36; CM 234.

First stanza, lines 3-4: 'would like to die, I know,/ it would please them to do it.' Refrain: 'wait and wait' rather than 'wait and see'.

32. B 755, V 358; JN[1] 190.

Difficult text to read. The idea of the two-word refrain seems to be 'it's finished', but the exact meaning of *çafar* is uncertain, and the word is written as *cafar* or *gafar* in B.

The 'cake' at the end is literally 'wedding bread', which might mean a cake, or might reflect the sentiment contained in a Portuguese proverb:

Marriage is a panada
you eat while it's still hot;
as long as the wedding bread lasts,
the bride jumps for joy.

(Cited by Lapa in *Miscelânea*, p.167.)

Second stanza literally reads:

Our great loves,
which you and I always had –
we never fully consummated them,
like Blanchefleur and Floris,
but the time of those who play
is over.

Third stanza, line 4-6: 'as long as the day lasted,/ but this, Don Joam Garcia,/ is over'.

33. B 1485, V 1097; RL 203.

Literal rendering of first stanza:

Ugly lady, you've complained
that I never praise you in my singing;
but now I wish to make a song
in which I'll praise you after all;
and you see how I wish to praise you:
ugly lady, old and crazy!

The last three lines of the next two stanzas read similarly to those of the first.

34. B 1498, V 1108; RL 212.

Second stanza, line 4: 'forever' rather than 'until she's dead'.

35. B 1490, V 1101; RL 207.

36. B 689, V 291; JN[1] 122.

The end of the refrain in the manuscripts reads 'fair and' *[louçana e]*, as if another adjective were meant to follow.

37. B 1511, RL 130.

Joam Soarez Coelho, in flagrant violation of the class-conscious code of courtly love, composed two *cantigas* for a nursemaid, thereby provoking a storm of satiric *cantigas* in response.

The last lines of the third stanza are obscure. The translation reflects the interpretation offered by Michaëlis and accepted by Lapa, but an etymological study is needed to clarify the meanings of several words.

38. B 1173, V 779; Reali, 'Juyão Bolseyro' 11.

An obscure word in the refrain, *lirias*, probably refers to some kind of musical embellishment. The refrain literally runs: 'he made *lirias* in the sound [music]/ that wrench my heart'. Third stanza, line 3: 'and for this I greatly thank him'.

39. B 1165, V 771; Reali, 'Juyão Bolseyro' 3.

Third stanza, lines 3 and 4: 'then the light that I don't want comes immediately,/ and the night goes away and [the light] comes and grows'.

40. B 1176, V 782; Reali, 'Juyão Bolseyro' 14.

Refrain: 'in the time when my friend [beloved]/ used to talk with me?'

41. B 1527; RL 163.

The next to the last line, missing in the original manuscript, was provided by Lapa.

42. B 1518; RL 154.

A number of Gil Perez Conde's *cantigas* derided the knights who refused to serve in the war against the Moorish king of Granada, who rose up against Alfonso X in the early 1260s. This *cantiga* seems to belong to that group, but the gist of the satire isn't clear. Was chicken, a mild meat, considered the food of weaklings and cowards? Or was the troubadour poking fun at some superstitious behaviour of the king?

43. B 1524; RL 160.

The humour of this *cantiga* turns on the ironic doubling of the possessive (*Thy my*...), the soldier's wages belonging to him by right but in fact still in the hands of the king.

44. B 1558; RL 60.

The cavalrymen that frightened the unidentified noble were the Zeneti, a Berber tribe famed for horsemanship. Many had come from North Africa to aid the Moors of Granada in their fight against the armies of Alfonso X (1261-65). The Zeneti rode on small saddle horses whose name – jennets – derived from that of the tribe. It's possible, in fact, that the third line of each stanza refers to the horses themselves rather than to their riders.

45. B 480, V 63; RL 10.

Difficult text to transcribe, to classify and to interpret. Michaëlis believed the author was speaking for someone else; Lapa and other scholars consider the *cantiga* autobiographical. Both points of view may be true. The king, whose reign had rather accentuated ups and downs, was no doubt feeling some of the disillusion expressed in these verses, and he may have spent time at sea as he certainly did in battle, but surely he was never obliged to work as a sentinel. (Third stanza, lines 5-7. There were Rules according to which knights were to wear their armour at night, but the king was no common knight, and line 7 clearly states that the narrator made rounds.) Autobiographical or not, the *cantiga* is unique, being neither a love song nor a satire, yet too personal and too melancholy to be considered a true sirvente.

Second stanza, lines 12-13: 'from the scorpions' poison,/ for I know no other remedy'. Third stanza, lines 5-7: 'and to go armed at night gives me no pleasure, nor to make rounds'.

46. E 10, T 10, To 10; WM 10.

Third stanza, line 4: 'that we do as sinners' instead of 'of our dark hours'. Fourth stanza, line 4: 'devil' instead of 'evil powers'. It's possible to interpret the phrase idiomatically as 'give it to the devil', an expression found in troubadour love poetry.

47. E 60, T 60, To 70; WM 60.

Refrain literally runs: 'Between Ave and Eve/ there's a great difference'. Note that the name 'Eva', in the original, is a perfect inversion of 'Ave', which of course designates the Virgin Mary.

48. E 103, T 103, To 93; WM 103.

Fourth stanza, line 3: 'do good works' instead of 'follow the Way'.

49. B 493, V 76; RL 23.

The last lines of the second stanza are somewhat obscure. Whereas the original simply states that aroused women resemble the designated animals, the translation offers a possible interpretation, supposing that the animals are in heat.

St Anthony's fire – known also as St Francis's fire, St Marcoul's fire, and the ignis sacer [holy fire] – is a highly infectious form of erysipelas that spread in epidemic proportions during the Middle Ages. The 91st *Song in Praise of Holy Mary* (WM 91) describes the devastating effects of this skin disease and the Virgin Mary's cure of it in France, where it killed thousands of people in the twelfth century.

Fourth stanza, line 7 (6 in the translation): 'he removes [exorcises] the wicked demon from her'.

50. R 1, B 1278, V 884; Ferreira, *Codax* 1.

The refrain literally reads 'And oh God, will he come soon?' or, if understood as an invocation: 'And oh God, may he come soon!' Third stanza: 'for whom I sigh' instead of 'who makes my heart troubled'.

51. R 2, B 1279, V 885; Ferreira 2.

52. R 3, B 1280, V 886; Ferreira 3, but with lines 8 and 11 according to JN[1] 493.

B and V present the third and fourth stanzas in reverse order, which is the normal order according to the rules of parallelism. But in V, as Ferreira points out on p.147, the copyist began to write the third and fourth stanzas in the 'wrong' order (as they appear here and in R), apparently 'correcting' the anomaly present in the source text.

Third stanza, line 2: 'and there, mother, my beloved will come'. Fourth stanza, line 2: 'and there, mother, my friend will come'.

53. R 4, B 1281, V 887; Ferreira 4.

Codax violates a rule of parallelism by switching the word order of the second line of the second stanza when it is repeated in the first line of the fourth stanza.

In the original, the second stanza restates the information of the first; God is not beseeched.

54. R 5, B 1282, V 888; Ferreira 5.

Line 1 of first and second stanzas: 'All [girls] who know how to love a friend/beloved'. Line 2 of third and fourth stanzas: 'and we will see my friend/beloved'.

55. R 6, B 1283, V 889; Ferreira 6.

As in No. 52, two of the parallelistic stanzas – three and four – are in reverse order. The recurrence of this anomaly, together with the anomaly present in No. 53, suggests that the poet acted deliberately.

In the first, second, fifth and sixth stanzas: 'in the churchyard' instead of 'by the belfry'. Refrain: 'I'm in love'.

56. R 7, B 1284, V 890; Ferreira 7.

57. B 852, V 438; JN[1] 252.

Tavani, in *Poesia Lírica*, pp.140-42, publishes this *cantiga* with a one-line refrain reading *Eu atendendo'o meu amigu'! E verrá?*, which would translate as: 'I waiting for my friend! And will he come?' Nunes understood the last three letters in the mss. – *eu a* – as indicating that the verse was to be repeated, but in fact there seems to be an abbreviation mark over the *u*, which is the basis for Tavani's very different reading.

The chapel of St Simon is on the island of the same name [San Simón], opposite Vigo on the Galician coast. At low tide one used to be able to reach the chapel on foot, though this is no longer possible.

The first two stanzas do not say she is actually praying. Third stanza, line 2 (and repeated in fifth stanza, line 1): 'I don't have a boatman, nor an oarsman.' Fourth stanza, line 2 (and repeated in sixth stanza, line 1): 'I don't have a boatman, and I don't know how to row.'

58. B 963, V 550; Rodríguez 24.

Second stanza, line 4: 'and turn from where he has great interests'.

59. B 1035, V 625; Rodríguez 55.

The second stanza in the translated version is considerably more colloquial than the original.

60. B 1024, V 614; Rodríguez 44.

61. B 965, V 552; Rodríguez 21.

62. B 967 (part), V 554; Rodríguez 23.

Crecente is located near Santiago de Compostela. The Sar is a small river. Exactly what the shepherdess is doing with her dress (actually a skirt) in line 5 is unclear, but the image seems to be borrowed from a pastoral by the Provençal troubadour Giraut de Bornelh (c.1162-1199). In the second stanza of his 'L'altrer, lo primer jorn d'aost', the shepherdess is also in some way pressing or being pressed by her skirt ('estrecha-lh gonela que vest'), while in the first stanza the narrator is struck – like Joam Airas's – by the song of a shepherdess in a wood next to a stream.

First stanza, line 3: the narrator may have been going on horse rather than foot; line 4: 'gently' not in the original. Second stanza, line 4: 'on the branches all around'.

63. B 1467, V 1077; Rodríguez 73.

In two other *cantigas* (V 601; B 1468/V 1078), Joam Airas satirizes the superstitious who believed crows were omens and useful for soothsaying. Here, of course, the crow is not a crow at all.

Third stanza, line 1: 'What will happen?' instead of 'Who'll save me?'; line 5: the crow's exclamation seems to be onomatopoeic but also might mean 'Here, here!' Fourth stanza, lines 3-4: 'she wanted to try to go,/ and there was a crow on top of her'.

64. B 1546; RL 245.

This is the same Maria Perez lampooned by Pero da Ponte (see No. 22 and corresponding note) and other troubadours.

Final stanza: 'Any man who wants to get on top/ of Maria Perez, take something underneath.' The unspecified something might mean money in his pocket, which would be consistent with the two previous stanzas, but it could also refer to his penis.

65. V 1035; Tavani, *Lourenço* 16.

This *tenção* is probably incomplete. According to Section 3, Chapter 7 of the *Arte de Trobar* (see Note 21), each of the two interlocutors should have equal time, but the sole surviving manuscript version of this *cantiga* does not give us Joam Vasquiz's second reply.

Second stanza, line 5: 'But tell me, you who produce [metrically] uneven verses'. In the third stanza Lourenço claims his verses are just as regular as Joam Vasquiz's.

66. B 1108, V 699; Zilli 6.

The fifth line of each stanza is consistently non-rhyming. This technique is identified in Section 4, Chapter 2 of the *Arte de Trobar* (see Note 21) as the *palavra perduda* [missing word], known in Provençal poetry as *rim estramp*.

67. B 1227, V 832; Zilli 14.

68. B 735, V 336; JN[1] 169.

Vale de Prados is in the northeast corner of Portugal. It was common practice to dance during pilgrimages and religious feasts, outside and sometimes even inside the church.

The translation puts the mothers 'in the chapel' and the girls 'on the steps', but the original has no such indications – they are simply all there at the shrine.

69. V 1027; RL 411, but with the fourth line as per the original ms. and with the eleventh line following the reading of Gonçalves, p.276.

Difficult text to transcribe. While the object of the satire is clear enough, the exact meaning of specific phrases must be guessed at. 'Rich man' was a title of nobility – see Note 24.

Literal rendering:

A rich man comes from [where] the trout [is sold],
having bought two as if that were a lot,
and he cooks one of them.

Although he likes black[?] fish,
he buys two little ones,
and he cooks one of them.

They sell a hundred lively trout,
and he buys two miserable ones,
and he cooks one of them.

And where they sell them twitching [fresh]
he goes away with two that are frying [not fresh],
and he cooks one of them.

The word for black in line 4 is ebony *[ebenas]* – could this have been used figuratively to mean 'attractive'? Gonçalves, p.276, suggests the copyist misread the word *cheas*, which meant full, plump, large.

70. B 1436, V 1046; RL 413.

71. B 1435, V 1045; RL 412.

72. B 903, V 488; JN[2] 153.

Literal version of stanzas (w/o the refrain):

Whenever I see the waves
and the very high shores,
waves immediately come
to my heart for the fair one.

I never see the waves
nor the very high rocks
without waves coming
into my heart for the lovely one.

If I see the waves
and I see the steep coasts,
waves immediately come
to my heart for the beautiful one.

73. B 901, V 486; CM 309.

This *cantiga* uses the poetic device known as *dobre* – word doubling – described in Section 4, Chapter 5 of the *Arte de Trobar* (see Note 21). The original repeats, in each stanza, the end word of the first verse in the fourth verse. The device employed in the translation more nearly resembles *mozdobre* (see Note 21), in which words are repeated in different forms.

The translation accentuates the playful tone of the original. Third stanza, line 4: 'But now it happens to me differently.' Fourth stanza: 'A man should not rejoice/ too much over what he can have,/ because I – who wanted to do just that – / have nothing now to rejoice over.'

74. B 810, V 394; JN[2] 119, correcting the eighth line according to B and V.

First stanza, line 4: 'I'll tell you what happens to me.' Second stanza, line 2: 'I'm dead, if I don't die soon.' Refrain: 'nor good nor bad' in lieu of 'nor faith nor doubt'. Third stanza, line 4: 'which I think is the greatest of all pains'.

75. A 251; CM 251.

Attribution to Pai Gomez Charinho is conjectural but generally accepted by scholars. The thematic material is typical of Charinho, and so are many of the technical aspects. Like No. 74, this *cantiga* employs enjambement between stanzas, as well as between the last stanza and a two-verse *fiinda* [envoi] at the end. Section 4, Chapter 3 of the *Arte de Trobar* (see Note 21) describes this as a special technique that holds the meaning in suspense, not allowing the song to close *ata a fiinda* [until the *fiinda*], so that scholars have adopted the term *atá-finda* for *cantigas* of this type.

Refrain, which is invariable: 'the pain of love makes me forget/ the very great pain of sea and [makes me] consider'. Second stanza, line 1: 'as the greatest of all pains'. Third stanza, line 1: 'as the greatest pain, I tell you truly'; line 4: 'say it's not [that way], but I'll say how it is'. Couplet: 'As the greatest pain that which makes [one] lose/ the pain of sea, which makes many die.'

76. B 817, V 401; JN[1] 220.

Critics have variously suggested that the flowers mentioned in the refrain might refer to the girl's parting gift to her beloved, to the fleurs-de-lis of his shield, or to fleurs-de-lis adorning the ship's banners.

Sixth stanza, line 2: 'a worthy figure [lovely girl]' instead of 'his lady'. The latter designation was used in the translation to indicate the courtly nature of the service mentioned in the same line.

77. B 838, V 424; JN[1] 221.

First stanza, line 1: '[female] friend' instead of 'sister'. Refrain, line 2: 'as he freed me from the pains of love, may God so free him'. Third stanza: 'How relieved I am, for now each time/ a man arrives from the border/ I won't be afraid that he brings me bad news./ Because he did good to me, without being asked.'

78. B 1211, V 816; JN[1] 334.

First stanza, line 2 (line 1 in the original): '[female] friend' instead of 'sister'. Refrain, line 2: 'let's talk about my friend'.

79. B 244 (first stanza), 246a (second and third stanzas); JN[2] 1.

An amended version of this *cantiga*, which may derive from the French medieval lays, appears in the *Amadis de Gaula*, a Peninsular romance that probably goes back to the thirteenth century. While the earliest surviving fragments (fifteenth century) and complete edition (that of Montalvo, 1508) of the romance were written in Spanish, there is good but inconclusive evidence that it was originally written in Portuguese, perhaps in part by Joam Lobeira himself and/or by a relative named Vasco de Lobeira.

The 'rosette' of the refrain is a literal, small rose rather than a rose-like ornament. Second stanza, line 6: 'I could kill a lion.'

80. A 142, B 263; CM 142.

The troubadour named in the first line is Joam Garcia de Guilhade (cf. No. 31). It is highly unusual for a *cantiga d'amor* to cite the admired lady by name. Guiomar Affonso Gata was the half-sister of Maria Pais Ribeirinha, a mistress of King Sancho I (cf. Note to No. 3).

The refrain literally reads:

'This is the death that kills:
Guiomar Affonso Gata
is the woman who kills me.'

81. A 143, B 264; CM 143.

82. B 1380, V 988; Blasco 47.

Literal version:

Roi Queimado died of love
in his cantigas, by Holy Mary,
for a woman whom he greatly loved;
and to appear all the more a troubadour
(because she wouldn't show him favour)

he made himself die in his cantigas,
but then rose up on the third day.

He did this for his lady
whom he greatly loves, and I'll tell you more:
because he thinks he shows great mastery
in the cantigas he composed
– dying in them and then returning to life –
he does this [feat] that he can do,
whereas no one else would do it for anything.

And he doesn't fear his death
(otherwise he would fear his death more)
but knows very well, being so clever,
that he will live after he has died,
and he makes himself die in his cantigas,
since he comes back to life, and you see what power
God has given him! Who could ever imagine!
And if God had given me this power
that he [Roi Queimado] has of living after dying,
I would never again fear death!

83. B 1383[2] [second of two *cantigas* numbered 1382, found on folios 295-96], V 992; Blasco 50, correcting the second line of the refrain according to B and V.

Lapa (RL, p.569) lamented the vulgarity of the last stanza, while another scholar spoke of its 'abrupt comic effect', but the stanza is not gratuitous and the comedy is not sudden. The difficulty centres around a misreading of the refrain. Lapa and succeeding editors declared the word *sorrabedes* (line 2 of the refrain) unintelligible, substituting it with various alternates deemed to make more sense. But as the medievalist José León Acosta points out in an unpublished note, the word *sorrabar* exists even today, being derived from *so* [under] + *rabo* [buttocks] and meaning to flatter or to fawn on or (to use an updated equivalent) to 'kiss ass'. The English rendering of the refrain attempts to catch the double joke: (1) the play on words – she 'after his ass' and he 'farting' in response – and (2) the reversal of the usual scenario of courtly love, since it is the woman rather than the man who must feel honoured on account of her love for him.

Refrain: 'If you love me,/ by God, [female] friend, you'll be after my ass today,/ if you love me.' Second stanza, lines 1-2: 'I did so much for your love/ when [*or* where] you set up a tryst with me.' Fourth stanza, lines 1-2: 'I evacuated farts for you/ when [*or* where] you set up a tryst with me.'

84. B 1384, V 993; Blasco 51.

The technical vocabulary of equine pathology is employed here. Blasco and other scholars suggest that the Maria Negra of this and the preceding *cantiga* is none other than Maria Perez Balteira (see Note 22), but this seems unlikely. By the time Pero Garcia de Burgalês began composing, the notorious singer-courtesan had already made her crusade or was talking about it, and the troubadours lost few opportunities to satirize her new-found religiosity. This is indeed what Pero Garcia satirizes in his one *cantiga* that names the Balteira (B 1374/V 982), whereas his three *cantigas* lampooning Maria Negra (B 1382/V 990 is the one not included here) simply focus on her nymphomania, with no implication of religious hypocrisy.

85. B 1379, V 987; Blasco 46.

This satire against Fernando Diaz's homosexuality turns on the phrase *vay sobr'el*, which means both *he goes after him* and *he goes on top of him*. The *meirinho* (rendered here as *sheriff*) was responsible for keeping law and order and settling legal disputes; he would go from town to town, looking out for the King's interests, which often had to compete with those of powerful nobles. Viveiro is a coastal town north of La Coruña; Carrion lies between León and Burgos.

First stanza, line 3: 'neighbour' rather than 'friend'. Second stanza, line 3: 'the King made him sheriff from Viveiro'.

86. B 1378, V 986; Blasco 45.

First stanza, line 2: 'now I wish to reveal to you'.

87. B 1377, V 985; Blasco 44.

Fernando Escalho was a jongleur, accused of too much sleeping and sexual activity in another of Pero Garcia's *cantigas* (B 1376/V 984). His practice of sodomy was alluded to in a *cantiga d'escarnho* by Pero D'Ambroa (B 1603/V 1135) and in another by Roi Paez Ribela (V 1026).

The English version is somewhat more colloquial, especially the last line of the first stanza, which literally reads: 'and therefore he lost all of his singing'.

88. B 135; CM 389, with changes in lines 19 and 41, as per Lapa, *Lições*, pp.147-48.

This is the best Galician-Portuguese example of the *descort* ['discord'], a Provençal form in which the stanzas varied in length, metre, rhyme and melody – hence the name. Nun'Eanes Cerzeo, as evidenced by the final line, saw in this form (or lack thereof) the perfect analogue for his existential discord. The pulsing rhythm and alternating line length that begin in the fifth stanza were typical of the *descort* and also of the *lay* (see No. 79). A *cantiga* by the Galician troubadour Lopo Lias (B 1355/V 963) has a similar rhythm and is identified in the Songbooks as a *descor*. A third example, a plaintive love song by Alfonso X (B 470), may also be considered a *descort*, although it is not so indicated in the Songbook.

First stanza, line 6: 'and I thank God because I'm leaving'. Fourth stanza, lines 5-6: 'but now I'll never be unhappy/ since I'm leaving [this land] and going on my way'. Eighth stanza, lines 6-10: 'May I be able to have strength and take pleasure, for this is what I will seek.'

89. A 305; Stegagno Picchio, *Martin Moya* 12.

The author of this and three other songs was long in doubt, but Stegagno Picchio presents convincing evidence for attributing them to Martin Moxa.

Second stanza, line 1: 'We have a false and tasteless world.' Third stanza, lines 3-4: 'What happened to love and troubadouring? Why do people/ look sad and no longer sing?' Next to last line: 'Why would a man of worth live'.

90. B 1151^2-1152^2 [found on folios 246-47], V 754; Cunha 2.

This *cantiga d'amor* is curious for having the compact, parallelistic form of a *cantiga d'amigo*.

91. B 1153, V 755; Cunha 3.

This *cantiga d'amigo* is unusual for being narrated exclusively from the mother's point of view. Notice its lexical similarity (in the original) with the previous *cantiga*.

92. B 1157, V 759; Cunha 4.

In the third stanza, *virgo* is a virgin but is used here to mean 'young girl' or 'maiden' more than to indicate sexual inexperience. Fourth stanza, line 3: 'to carry a young noblewoman'.

93. B 1154, V 756; Cunha 11.

The meaning of this *cantiga* becomes clearer if one considers that long hair was associated with maidenhood in Galician-Portuguese troubadour poetry. Cf. No. 13, No. 36 and No. 99.

94. B 1158, V 760; Cunha 5.

First line of both stanzas: 'shore' instead of 'bend'.

95. B 879, V 462; Tavani, *Ayras Nunez* 7.

Nunez's *cantiga d'amigo* is a reworked version of one by Joam Zorro (B 1158, V 761). Some scholars have suggested that both versions were adaptations of an already existing *cantiga d'amigo* of popular origin. This could be true for Joam Zorro, but Airas Nunez made a habit of borrowing from his fellow troubadours, and another of his *cantigas* (a pastoral, B 868-869-870/V 454) likewise 'quotes' from a Joam Zorro *cantiga*. Such borrowing, far from being considered plagiarism, was a respected part of a good troubadour's art. The ninth chapter of the *Arte de Trobar* (see Note 21) describes the *cantiga de seguir* ('*cantiga* that follows') as one in which the troubadour imitates some aspect of a preexisting *cantiga* by using (1) the same melody and metre, (2) the same melody and rhyme, or (3) the same words of a stanza to mean – if he is clever enough – something different. The *cantiga de seguir* could serve to parody a preexisting *cantiga*, to improve on it, or merely to offer a technically achieved variation – a kind of parallelism, but from *cantiga* to *cantiga* rather than from stanza to stanza.

Literal rendering:

Let us all three dance, dear [girl]friends,
under these flowering hazel trees,
and whoever is pretty like us, [who are] pretty,
if she loves a [boy]friend,
under these flowering hazel trees
will come to dance.

Let us all three dance, dear sisters,
under this branch of these hazel trees,
and whoever is fair like us, [who are] fair,
if she loves a [boy]friend,
under this branch of these hazel trees
will come to dance.

By God, dear friends, as long as we're doing nothing else
let us dance under this flowering branch,
and whoever looks comely as we look,
if she loves a [boy]friend,
under this branch – under which we dance –
will come to dance.

96. B 871, V 455; Tavani 2.

Cistercium is the Medieval Latin name for the town of Cîteaux, where the Cistercian Order was founded by reformist Benedictines in 1098.

The translation guesses at what the original might have been for the missing sixth line of the second stanza. Third stanza, lines 1-2: 'And in Cistercium, where truth/ had always lived...' Fourth stanza, last line: 'for no one here has any news of her'.

97. B 872, V 456; Tavani 3.

First stanza, line 2: 'for these branches and for these flowers'. First line of closing couplet: 'I have great ardour and great joy.'

98. B 1192, V 797; Azevedo Filho 9.

99. B 1188, V 793; Azevedo Filho 5.

First stanza, line 2 (and in third stanza, line 1): '...to the cold spring...' Second stanza, line 2 (and in fourth stanza, line l): 'she goes to wash her hair in the cold spring'. All stanzas mix present and past verb tenses.

100. B 569, V 172; JN[1] 20.

Obviously inspired by No. 99, Dinis's version is a masterpiece of rhythmic sensibility and semantic complexity. The entire *cantiga* turns on the recurring word *alva*, which can mean 'white, pure', but also 'dawn, daybreak'. Thus the second line of each stanza may mean that the girl woke up 'white and pure', or that she woke up at dawn; or perhaps both meanings are intended. In the fifth line of each verse, it seems clear that the girl washes the shirts 'white'. And in the third line of the last two stanzas, *alva* is again used as she 'turns white with rage'.

101. B 568, V 171; JN[1] 19.

The fifth stanza is missing from the Songbooks but is easily reconstructed on account of the parallelistic structure.

Fifth stanza, line 2 (and in seventh stanza, line 1): 'he's well and alive' instead of 'he's well, he's coming'. Sixth stanza, line 2 (and in eighth stanza, line 1): 'he's alive and well' instead of 'he's coming, he's well'. Seventh stanza, line 2 (and eighth stanza, line 2): 'and he'll be with you within the time he promised'.

102. B 572, V 176; JN^{1} 24.

Second line of refrain: *'– I'll do it, friend, doing my best.'*

103. B 1539; RL 94.

The first two verses of each stanza are rather flatter in the original, saying merely that the narrator got very bored from hearing his unidentified guest talk so much. Third stanza, line 3: 'and he didn't know if [his talk] was bad [uninteresting] or good [interesting]'.

104. B 520^{3} [the last of three *cantigas* numbered 520, found on folio 118], V 123; JN^{2} 69.

Third stanza, lines 1-4: 'For God never put anything bad in my lady/ but put beauty and worthiness in her/ and made her talk well and laugh better/ than any other woman...'

105. B 524^{3} [found on folios 118-19], V 127; JN^{2} 73.

First stanza, lines 4-5: '...do not/ have such great pain in their heart/ as I see myself bear for my lady'. Second stanza: 'Although they make verses and know how to praise/ their ladies as much and as well/ as they can, I know/ that those who make verses when the flower is in season/ and not otherwise, if God excuse me,/ do not have the unequalled pain that I have.' Third stanza, lines 5-6: '...do not live in that perdition/ in which I now live and that is bound to kill me'.

106. B 514, V 97; JN^{2} 45.

107. B 543, V 146; JN^{2} 91.

108. B 534, V 137; JN^{1} 2.

The question in the second stanza is actually directed to the shepherdess's absent lover. Fourth stanza, line 6: 'do not complain' instead of 'have some faith and courage'.

109. B 720, V 321; JN^{1} 155.

This is the only Galician-Portuguese evocation of the *chanson de toile*, a medieval French song in which an enamoured girl tells of her love while weaving or embroidering. The last line here is based on the belief that vulture meat conferred divinatory powers.

First stanza, line 2: 'reciting' instead of 'singing'. Second stanza, line 2: 'singing' instead of 'humming'. Third stanza: '...I know you have/ an impassioned love, so well do you recite/ songs of love'. Fourth stanza: '...I know you are/ passionately in love, so well do you sing/ songs of love'.

110. B 1298, V 902; Toriello 6.

First stanza, line 1: 'rest' instead of 'sit'. Second stanza, line 1: 'relax' instead of 'walk'. Third stanza, line 2 (again in line 2 of the fourth stanza and in line 1 of the fifth and sixth stanzas): 'his bow in hand shooting at birds'. Sixth stanza, line 2: 'and he doesn't wish to kill those that sing'.

111. B 1604 (part), V 1136; Toriello 8.

112. B 1606, V 1139; Stegagno Picchio, *Lição*, pp.85-86.

The middle stanza is missing from the Songbooks. Elvas is a fortified Portuguese town that borders on Spain.

First stanza, line 6: *lançado* is understood here as 'cast [out]' but could also mean 'wounded by a lance' (see Stegagno Picchio, ibid., pp.91-92); lines 7-8: 'that leaves the world to be lost/ from the company of the does'. Refrain, line 2: 'under the influence of plants'. Second stanza, line 3: 'sensible' instead of 'fine'.

113. B 416, V 27; RL 66. This *cantiga* is also found on two loose sheets from the seventeenth century: (M) folio 25 r° of volume CC99 in the National Library of Madrid, and (P) an unnumbered folio from volume 419 of the Municipal Library of Oporto.

The first four stanzas have been reduced from 7 to 6 lines without excluding any information except at the end of the second stanza where V. Martins says 'and that is all you need to know from me', and towards the end of the fourth stanza, where he affirms that the lady in question 'conquers all others in terms of beauty'. Closing triplet: the lady is 'alive and full of good sense'.

About the Galician-Portuguese Troubadours

AFONS'EANES DO COTON was a Galician noble who apparently fell on hard times, taking refuge in various Spanish courts and specializing in satiric, often pornographic songs. According to King Alfonso X (in B 485/V 68), the younger troubadour Pero da Ponte learned from Afonso do Coton and stole some of his verses. *Nos. 11-12.*

AFONSO MENDEZ DE BESTEIROS may have been one of the Portuguese nobles to take refuge in the Castilian court after the fall of Sancho II in 1248. He apparently fought in the expeditions of Alfonso X against the Moors. *No. 44.*

AFONSO SANCHEZ (1279?-1329) was the oldest and the favourite among King Dinis's nine bastard sons. The one legitimate son, Afonso IV, was so jealous that he rebelled against him and against the King. Afonso Sanchez took refuge in Castile and subsequently invaded northern Portugal. It was only through the persistent intervention of Isabel, the Queen mother, that the half brothers were finally reconciled. *No. 113.*

AIRAS NUNEZ was a cleric, perhaps from Santiago de Compostela, who served in the Castilian court of Sancho IV from 1284-1289. His poems were strongly influenced by Provençal poetry, and though limited in number (15 survive), they touched a wide variety of themes. He almost certainly collaborated with Alfonso X on the *Cantigas de Santa Maria* and may actually have composed the larger part of them. *Nos. 95-97.*

ALFONSO X, KING OF CASTILE AND LEON (1221-1284) produced a vast body of historical and scientific prose in Spanish but wrote his poetry in Galician-Portuguese. Besides his contributions to the profane troubadour tradition, Alfonso X 'the Learned' compiled the *Cantigas de Santa Maria*, a collection of 427 songs – many written by him – in praise of the Virgin Mary. (See the Introduction.) *Nos. 45-49.*

DINIS served as king of Portugal from 1279 until his death in 1325. A great patron of national culture, he founded his country's first university in 1290 – transferred from Lisbon to Coimbra in 1308 – and was himself one of the most prolific and talented poets of the Galician-Portuguese school. No less than 137 of his *cantigas* have been preserved in the Songbooks. *Nos. 100-108.*

ESTEVAN COELHO, of whom only two *cantigas* survive, was active in the first part of the fourteenth century. He was the grandson of Joam Soarez Coelho, another Portuguese troubadour. *No. 109.*

FERNAND'ESQUIO tells us, in one of his nine surviving *cantigas*, that he was a soldier from Santiago de Compostela. Active around the year 1300, he was one of the last Galician-Portuguese troubadours. *Nos. 110-11.*

FERNAN GARCIA ESGARAVUNHA came from the Sousa family, one of the most powerful in Portugal's aristocracy. His *cantigas* date from the middle of the thirteenth century. His father and father-in-law were also poets. *No. 37.*

FERNAN RODRIGUEZ DE CALHEIROS was a knight, according to a note that precedes his *cantigas d'amigo* in the Songbook of the National Library (B). His position in the Songbooks suggests that he composed his *cantigas* in the early part of the thirteenth century. *Nos. 6-7.*

GIL PEREZ CONDE was of Portuguese origin but associated himself with the Castilian court some time before 1250 and later fought with Alfonso X against the Moors in southern Spain. Nearly all of this poet's 18 surviving *cantigas* were satirical. *Nos. 41-43.*

GIL SANCHEZ (d.1236), a bastard son of King Sancho I, was a renowned cleric and one of the first Galician-Portuguese troubadours. Only one *cantiga* is attributed to him. *No. 4.*

JOAM AIRAS DE SANTIAGO was, as his name indicates, from Santiago de Compostela, but he frequented the Castilian court of Alfonso X as well as the Portuguese court of Afonso III (1248-1279). Joam Airas was one of the most prolific and varied *cantiga* writers, with 81 surviving compositions. *Nos. 58-63.*

JOAM BAVECA's last name – probably a nickname – means 'fool', and a number of troubadours mocked his compositional capacities, all of which suggests that he was a jongleur by profession. Of Galician origin, he was associated with the Castilian court of Alfonso X. *Nos. 66-67.*

JOAM GARCIA DE GUILHADE was a low-ranking noble (a knight, he informs us in one of his *cantigas*) who made a living as a troubadour, apparently employing jongleurs to propagate his songs. Active in the mid-thirteenth century, the heyday of the Galician-Portuguese school, Joam de Guilhade was one of its most prolific and inventive poets, with 54 surviving *cantigas* that employ a number of original images and large doses of irony. His name appears in a number of his *cantigas*, usually to poke fun at himself. *Nos. 26-35.*

JOAM LOBEIRA was a Portuguese knight who served the kings Afonso III (1248-1279) and Dinis (1279-1325). Seven of his *cantigas* have come down to us. *No. 79.*

JOAM SOAREZ COELHO, from a noble Portuguese family of considerable wealth, seems to have preferred travelling and art to business. He spent most of his youth abroad, in Spain and possibly in Provence as well. Somewhere along the way, perhaps in the Castilian court of Ferdinand III, he may have met the Italian troubadour Sordello (mentioned in Dante's *Divine Comedy*). Joam Soarez served as counsellor to Afonso III from 1250 to 1279, but even then he was often away from his post and from Portugal. Fifty-two of his *cantigas* were recorded in the Songbooks. *No. 36.*

JOAM VASQUIZ DE TALAVEIRA was from Castile, and we know from information in his *cantigas* that he was active in the second half of the thirteenth century, serving both Alfonso X and his successor, Sancho IV. *Nos. 64-65.*

JOAM ZORRO's biography is a mystery. The fact his texts mention Lisbon and the King of Portugal (Dinis?) suggests he was Portuguese. His eleven surviving songs are mostly concerned with the sea, and all but one (No. 102) are *cantigas d'amigo*. *Nos. 90-94.*

JUIÃO BOLSEIRO's last name means 'purse-maker' or perhaps 'treasurer', suggesting in either case that he was of humble origin. Active in the third quarter of the thirteenth century, he seems to have been a jongleur in the service of Mem Rodriguez Tenoiro, a Galician troubadour. *Nos. 38-40.*

LOPO was a Galician jongleur, probably in the service of Ferdinand III, King of Castile-Leon from 1230 to 1252. According to fellow troubadour Martin Soarez, Lopo sang and played abominably, though Soarez's satiric *cantigas* admit that Lopo wrote good lyrics. *No. 8.*

LOURENÇO was a jongleur who played the cither. He was for a time in the service of Joam Garcia de Guilhade and eventually tried his own hand at composing, producing seven *cantigas d'amigo*, two *cantigas d'amor* and one *cantiga d'escarnho*. A number of indignant troubadours scorned his pretensions to their art, giving rise to various dialogued songs (see Introduction about the *tenção*) in which Lourenço defends himself against charges of compositional mediocrity. *No. 65.*

MARTIN CODAX may have been a Galician jongleur, active in the second half of the thirteenth century. His seven *cantigas d'amigo* seem to be related, telling the story of a girl's first love. Numbers 1 through 5 and number 7 are of particular interest for being almost the only *cantigas* whose musical notation has come down to us. *Nos. 50-56.*

MARTIN MOXA was a cleric attached to the Castilian court of Alfonso X. His twenty surviving *cantigas* reveal a poet of considerable erudition, much influenced by the Provençal troubadours. *No. 89.*

MARTIN SOAREZ, active from around 1230 to some time after 1250, was considered the greatest Galician-Portuguese troubadour of his day. He was from the Portuguese town of Ponte de Lima, near the Galician border, but seems to have spent time in the Spanish courts, where he met Provençal troubadours and adapted their comparatively sophisticated models to Peninsular poetry. *Nos. 9-10.*

MEENDINHO was presumably Galician. The diminutive form of his name and the absence of a surname suggest the humble origin of a jongleur. His single surviving *cantiga* evokes an aura of mystery sufficient to place him among the greatest Galician-Portuguese lyricists. *No. 57.*

NUN'EANES CERZEO's origins and destiny are a complete mystery. Nine of his *cantigas* are extant. *No. 88.*

NUNO FERNANDEZ TORNEOL informs us, in one of his 22 *cantigas*, that he was a knight in the service of a Castilian noble who paid him with nothing but lies and deceit. *Nos. 17-18.*

OSOIR'ANES studied in Paris, which may explain why he composed elegant *cantigas d'amor* but no *cantigas d'amigo*, the more characteristically Iberian variety of song. He was a canon in the collegiate church of Santiago de Compostela. Named in his father's will, written in 1220, and having made a will of his own in 1236, the poet clearly belongs to the early period of Peninsular troubadour poetry. *No. 5.*

PAI GOMEZ CHARINHO (1225?-1295), a Galician noble from Pontevedra, served the kings Alfonso X and Sancho IV. He was Admiral over the Castilian navy, and the verses of his 28 *cantigas* often refer to the ocean. He was knifed to death by a close relative, apparently for political reasons. *Nos. 74-77.*

PAI SOAREZ DE TAVEIRÓS belonged to a leading family of Portuguese nobles. His *cantigas* are among the oldest we have, dating from around 1200. *Nos. 2-3.*

PEDR'AMIGO DE SEVILHA was a Galician cleric who spent time in King Alfonso X's court before serving as a canon in the cathedrals of Oviedo and Salamanca. He was called 'of Seville' because he presumably lived there as well. His name appears as a signing witness of a will from that city drawn up in 1285. He drew up his own will in 1302. He was one of the more prolific troubadours, with 36 extant *cantigas*. *No. 78.*

PEDR'EANES SOLAZ displayed considerable originality in his seven *cantigas* that have come down to us. He is thought to have been Galician, but nothing is known about him for sure. *No. 19.*

PERO DA PONTE authored at least 53 *cantigas*, many of which refer to the events of his time, as in several songs dealing with the defeat of the Moors in Valencia (1238) and Seville (1248). He had a flair for satiric songs, no doubt inherited from Afons'Eanes do Coton, his recognized master. *Nos. 20-25.*

PERO GARCIA BURGALÊS, as his name indicates, was from Burgos, Spain, but he travelled around, frequenting the courts of Alfonso X in Castile and Afonso III in Lisbon. He was a prolific poet, with fifty-three *cantigas*, including many notable satires. *Nos. 82-87.*

PERO GARCIA D'AMBROA was from the province of La Coruña in Galicia. He composed his *cantigas*, nearly all of them satiric, around the middle of the thirteenth century (he died in 1261), and probably frequented the court of Alfonso X. His fellow troubadours ridiculed him for not fulfilling a vow to make a pilgrimage to Jerusalem. According to Gonçal'Eanes do Vinhal (V 1004), Pero Garcia was afraid of the sea and so got no farther than Montpellier. *No. 13.*

PERO GOMEZ BARROSO was the bastard son of a Portuguese noble and a squire's daughter, but he managed to do better than his legitimate half brothers. He fought in the conquest of Seville from the Moors (1248) and served as Alfonso X's intermediary to pacify rebellious nobles in Granada (1273). *No. 14.*

PERO GONÇALVEZ DE PORTO CARREIRO, born into a noble family from northern Portugal, immigrated to Castile, where he frequented Alfonso X's court. His surviving output is limited to four *cantigas d'amigo*. *No. 16.*

PERO MAFALDO lampooned Pero Garcia d'Ambroa and Maria Perez Balteira (see Note for No. 22) in several of his nine *cantigas*, so we can assume he was associated with the court of Alfonso X. *No. 15.*

PERO MEOGO was a Galician, active in the thirteenth century. All nine of his *cantigas d'amigo* are graced by the presence of a mountain stag, which most critics consider a symbol of male sexuality. *Nos. 98-99.*

PERO VIVIAEZ is thought to have been a Galician jongleur of the thirteenth century, but nothing is known for sure. *No. 68.*

ROI FERNANDEZ was a clergyman from Santiago de Compostela. One of his *cantigas* suggests that he accompanied Fernando III's army when it captured Seville from the Moors. *Nos. 72-73.*

ROI PAEZ DE RIBELA, a master of short verses, may have been from Galicia or from Portugal, as there are various towns called Ribela on both sides of the Minho River. From allusions in his *cantigas*, we can assume that he frequented the court of Alfonso X. *Nos. 69-71.*

ROI QUEIMADO was of Portuguese origin, active in the second half of the thirteenth century. Twenty-four of his *cantigas* were recorded in the Songbooks. *Nos. 80-81.*

SANCHO I (1154-1211) was the second king of Portugal, assuming the throne in 1185, and his verses may be the oldest in Galician-Portuguese to have survived. A great fan of falconry and bullfighting, the king was also a fervent supporter of the arts. One of his sons, Gil Sanchez, was also a poet. *No. 1.*

VASCO MARTINS DE RESENDE left only one known *cantiga*, dating from the early part the fourteenth century. He was from an illustrious Portuguese family, which probably included Garcia de Resende, compiler of the *Cancioneiro Geral*, a collection of songs composed toward the end of the Middle Ages. *No. 113.*

VIDAL is identified in the Songbooks as 'the Jew from Elvas'. The manuscript note preceding his two *cantigas d'amor*, both of which are incomplete, makes a point of justifying the inclusion of a Jewish troubadour (who sang to a Jewish lady), saying that 'it's good not to let the good things a man produces be lost.' He was one of the last troubadours. *No. 112.*

Index of English Titles and First Lines